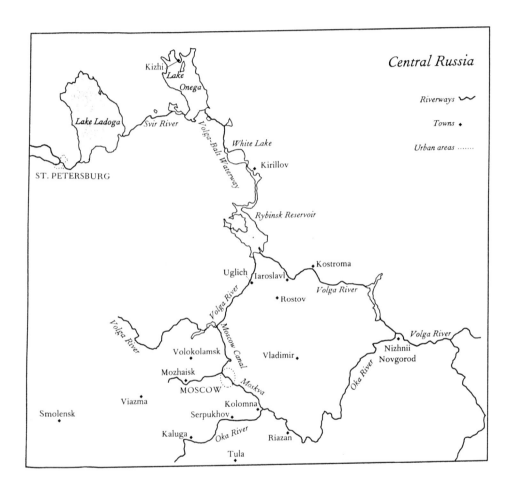

Central Russia

Riverways

Towns •

Urban areas ....

Kizhi

Lake Onega

Lake Ladoga

Svir River

Volga-Balt Waterway

White Lake

Kirillov

ST. PETERSBURG

Rybinsk Reservoir

Kostroma

Uglich

Iaroslavl

Volga River

Volga River

Rostov

Volga River

Moscow Canal

Volokolamsk

Vladimir

Nizhnii
Novgorod

Volga River

Mozhaisk

Oka River

MOSCOW

Moskva

Viazma

Kolomna

Smolensk

Serpukhov

Kaluga

Oka River

Riazan

Tula

Nizhnii Novgorod   Stroganov Church of the Nativity. 1685–1719. Southeast view.

Landmarks of
Russian Architecture

Documenting the Image

A series edited by
Helene E. Roberts, *Visual Resources, Dartmouth College, Hanover, New Hampshire,* and Brent Maddox, *J. Paul Getty Center for the History of Art and the Humanities, Santa Monica, California*

Documenting the Image describes the history, influences, and implications of visual artifacts. Its goals include publishing monographs and reference books that promote visual collections around the world.

Volume 1
An Introduction to Iconography: Symbols, Allusions and Meaning in the Visual Arts
Roelof van Straten
Translated by Patricia de Man

Volume 2
Art History through the Camera's Lens
Edited by Helene E. Roberts

Volume 3
"Remove Not the Ancient Landmark": Public Monuments and Moral Values
Edited by Donald M. Reynolds

Volume 4
"A Higher Branch of the Art": Photographing the Fine Arts in England, 1839–1880
Anthony J. Hamber

Volume 5
Landmarks of Russian Architecture: A Photographic Survey
William Craft Brumfield

Additional titles forthcoming

Landmarks of Russian Architecture

A Photographic Survey

Text and photographs by

William Craft Brumfield

Tulane University
New Orleans, Louisiana

Gordon and Breach Publishers

Australia • Canada • China • France • Germany • India • Japan • Luxembourg • Malaysia
• The Netherlands • Russia • Singapore • Switzerland • Thailand • United Kingdom

Amsteldijk 166
1st Floor
1079 LH Amsterdam
The Netherlands

Cover: *Viazma. Church of the Hodigitria Icon, Monastery of John the Baptist. 1635–38. Southeast view. William Craft Brumfield.*

British Library Cataloguing in Publication Data

Brumfield, William C. (William Craft), 1944–
   Landmarks of Russian architecture : a photographic survey.
   – (Documenting the image ; v.   5)
   1. Architecture, Russian – History   2. Architecture, Russian –
   Pictorial works
   I. Title
   720.9'47

ISBN 90-5699-537-5

CONTENTS

Introduction to the Series   vi

Preface   vii

1 Introductory Survey   1

2 Russian Wooden Architecture   9

3 Early Medieval Kiev   31

4 Novgorod: 11th–14th Centuries   37

5 The Vladimir Area: 11th–13th Centuries   49

6 Medieval Muscovy: 15th–16th Centuries   65

7 The Seventeenth Century   111

8 Eighteenth Century Baroque   147

9 Neoclassicism   165

10 Nineteenth Century Eclecticism   199

11 Twentieth Century   211

Illustrated Architectural Elements   235

Index   239

INTRODUCTION TO THE SERIES

Documenting the Image is devoted to describing the history, process, and use of visual documents. As many events and most artifacts are known and studied through images made of them, the study of the creation, collection, and use of these images becomes crucial to our understanding of the originals. *Documenting the Image* will provide an arena for discussion of the influence of visual documentation on culture, academic disciplines, and ways of thinking. It will inquire into how visual language is structured and how visual meaning is communicated. It will explore the visual documentation of artifacts through drawings, casts, facsimiles, engravings, and photography, and it will describe the effects of the new electronic technology on visual resources. Through the publication of catalogs of visual materials, it will seek to make these collections better known and more accessible to a wide range of potential users. In addition, the series will provide reference tools which support the description, organization, and use of visual collections.

PREFACE

Over the past decade Russian architecture has become the subject of increasing attention in the West. Yet there remains a need for a well-illustrated volume on its historical development that is accessible, in price and format, for students and teachers interested in the topic, as well as for the traveler to Russia. This book is intended to meet that need.

My survey concentrates on the European part of Russia, together with a few early medieval churches in the Ukraine. In choosing photos I have included not only obvious sites such as Moscow, St. Petersburg, Vladimir, and Novgorod, but also several provincial cities that I have only been able to photograph during the past few years. These photographs are representative of my work in Russia from the early 1970s to the present. This material is now held in the Photographic Archives of the National Gallery of Art in Washington, D.C., and I would like to acknowledge the cooperation of its staff. In addition, the Samuel H. Kress Foundation, New York, has provided generous support toward the preparation of my photographs for publication. I am also grateful to Helene Roberts—editor of the journal *Visual Resources* and of the *Documenting the Image* series of which this book forms a volume—for her support of photographic documentation in the arts.

The majority of monuments included in this book are churches, because Russian masonry architecture until the eighteenth century was largely a matter of churches, monasteries, and fortresses. Much has already been published in English on Soviet architecture, as well as on the imperial monuments of St. Petersburg. Therefore, my goal is to *illustrate* significant but less well-known monuments that reflect the entire sweep of Russian cultural history. Indeed, most Russians themselves are more aware of their medieval churches as "monuments" than they are of the buildings of the Russian avant garde.

As a photographic survey of Russian architectural history, the volume's organization is primarily chronological; yet geography also plays a role in revealing the continuity of local developments. In the section on medieval Muscovite architecture, I have arranged the material to illustrate the influence of Moscow's architectural culture on that of other Russian cities. In sections on the eighteenth and nineteenth centuries, both chronological and stylistic factors guide the presentation of the photographs. Whatever the period, it is hoped that the images and commentary will assist the student or traveler in understanding the historical and aesthetic significance of Russian architecture in its remarkable variety.

1. INTRODUCTORY SURVEY

MEDIEVAL PERIOD: 11TH–17TH CENTURIES

Very little is known of pre-Christian architecture among the eastern Slavs; but with the acceptance of Orthodox Christianity by Prince Vladimir of Kiev in 988, the construction of masonry churches spread throughout the territory of ancient Rus, as Byzantine clerics, artists, and builders were invited to the area. The largest and most complex of these early churches was Kiev's Cathedral of Divine Wisdom (1037–1050s), commissioned by Yaroslav the Wise and built with the direction of Greek masters. The interior contained extensive mosaics as well as frescoes. Other major churches of this period include the Sophia Cathedral in Novgorod (1045–1052), the Cathedral of the Transfiguration of the Savior in Chernigov (1031–1050s), and the Cathedral of the Dormition at the Kiev Cave Monastery (1073–1078; destroyed in 1941). Typically, these churches were built of opus mixtum (a combination of narrow brick, stone, and a mortar of crushed brick and lime). The application of stucco to church walls began toward the end of the twelfth century.

Regardless of size, the churches adhered to a plan known as the "inscribed cross," consisting of a cuboid core structure with crossing main aisles whose intersection was marked by the central dome, elevated on a cylinder supported by the four main piers. The interior bays were delineated on the exterior by pilasters culminating in curved gables known as *zakomary*, whose shape reflected the barrel vaulting of the interior. This cross-inscribed plan proved remarkably durable and capable of elaboration in small measure due to the iconographic system of frescoes that emphasized key points of the structure and gave the viewer clear reference points to the meaning of the church and its physical structure. Medieval chronicle references to architects are extremely rare, and in no case is there substantive information about any of the builders of medieval Russian churches.

In addition to Kiev, Novgorod, and neighboring cities, the third center of architecture in pre-Mongol Rus was the Vladimir-Suzdal principality, whose limestone churches were distinguished by carved decoration and precision of design. Grand Prince Yury Dolgoruky commissioned the first of these churches, such as the Transfiguration in Pereslavl-Zalessky (1152–1157). His son Andrei Bogoliubsky began the great era of limestone building in this area with the Cathedral of the Dormition, Vladimir (1158–1160); his palace church at Bogoliubovo (1158–1165) of which only fragments extant); and the Church of the Intercession (*Pokrov*) on the Nerl (1165). His successor, Vsevolod III, enlarged the Dormition Cathedral (1185–1189), and built the Cathedral of St. Dmitry in Vladimir (1194–1197), whose upper tier is covered with elaborate carving representing Biblical and secular motifs. Other churches of this period include the Cathedral of the Nativity of the Virgin in Suzdal (1222–1225) and St. George in Yurev-Polskoy (1234), both of which collapsed in the fifteenth century and were substantially reconstructed.

After the Mongol invasion of 1237–1241, church construction sharply declined. By the middle of the fourteenth century masonry construction revived, particularly in Novgorod with the support of wealthy merchants and neighborhood craft guilds. The Church of St. Theodore Stratilates on the Brook (1360–1361) and the Church of Transfiguration on Elijah Street (1374; frescoes by Theophanes the Greek) exemplified a distinct local style with steeply-pitched trefoil roofs. Moscow also enjoyed an architectural revival in the construction of limestone churches, but not until the last quarter of the fifteenth century did the major monuments of the Kremlin take shape under the direction of Italian masters imported by Ivan III.

In building the Dormition Cathedral (1475–1479), Aristotele Fioravanti introduced both a rigorously geometric plan and technical improvements such as deep foundation trenches with oak pilings, strong brick for the vaulting, and iron tie-rods. The interior, devoid of the usual choir gallery and with round columns, seemed unusually spacious and well lit. Brick soon displaced limestone for most masonry construction. Aleviz Novy used it in his Cathedral of the Archangel Michael (1505–1509), which had a number of Italianate elements. Italian influence also appeared in Marco Friazin and Pietro Antonio Solari's design of the Faceted Palace (1487–1491), and in the Kremlin walls and towers (1485–1516), built by Antonio Friazin, Marco Friazin, Solari, and others, with additions in the seventeenth century. The dominant element of the Kremlin, the Bell tower of Ivan the Great, was constructed in two stages: the lower two tiers in 1505–1508 by Bon Friazin, and the upper tier with cupola in 1599–1600.

During the sixteenth century, Moscow's brick votive churches displayed boldly inventive designs, also with Italian influence. The Church of the Ascension at Kolomenskoe (1530–1532) defined the "tent" (*shatior*) tower form, while the Decapitation of John the Baptist at Diakovo (ca. 1550) exemplified another form of the tower church. These prototypes were combined in the most spectacular and most famous of Russian churches, the Intercession on the Moat, popularly known as Vasily (Basil) the Blessed (1555–1561). Built in Red Square to celebrate Ivan IV's conquest of Kazan and Astrakhan, the structure consists of a central tent tower (dedicated to the Intercession of the Mother of God) surrounded by eight tower churches. Polychrome onion domes were added at the turn of the seventeenth century, while attached structures and much of the painted decoration appeared throughout the seventeenth century. The latter part of the sixteenth century also witnessed the building of major brick fortresses, most notably the citadel at Smolensk (1595–1602) by Fedor Kon.

After the depredations of the Time of Troubles (1605–1612), the building of masonry churches occurred on an unprecedented scale during the long reign of

Tsar Aleksei (1645–1676). Of special note are two large complexes: Patriarch Nikon's New Jerusalem (or Resurrection) Monastery west of Moscow, with a cathedral (1658–85) based on the plan of Jerusalem's Holy Sepulchre church; and in Rostov, Metropolitan Jonah Sysoevich's walled ensemble of churches and residence chambers (1670–1683). In a related development, many of Moscow's monasteries (Novodevichy, Novospassky, Simonov, Donskoy, Andronikov) were rebuilt in the late seventeenth century as was the great Trinity-Sergius Lavra (monastery) at Sergiev Posad forty-four miles (70 km) to the northeast. The proliferation of lavishly ornamented churches occurred throughout Muscovy, especially in Yaroslavl.

As Russia experienced increased contact with the West through Ukraine and northern Europe, elements of the Baroque appeared in numerous churches commissioned primarily by the Naryshkin and Sheremetev families on estates surrounding Moscow. Examples of the "Naryshkin Baroque" show a revival of the tower church form, often on a quatrefoil base as in the Churches of the Intercession at Fili (1690–1699), the Trinity at Troitskoe-Lykovo (1698–1703), and the Transfiguration at Ubory (1694–1697). The latter two churches are attributed to Yakov Bukhvostov, who also built the monumental Dormition Cathedral in Riazan (1693–1699). During the seventeenth century the use of brick in secular construction increased, mainly in Moscow, with its brick residences (*palaty*) and the tiered Sukharev Tower (1692–1701).

IMPERIAL PERIOD: 18TH–20TH CENTURIES

The assimilation of western architectural motifs increased radically during the reign of Peter I (1694–1725). In 1703 he founded St. Petersburg, which became the Russian capital in 1711. Architects imported from the western Europe, Jean Baptiste Le Blond (1679–1719) and Domenico Trezzini (1670–1734), submitted plans for its development. Le Blond's influence was substantial in defining the early Baroque in Petersburg, but his early death precluded a greater architectural legacy. Trezzini had a prolific career that included monuments such as the Cathedral of SS. Peter and Paul (1712–1732), the Building of the Twelve Colleges (1722–1741), Peter I's Summer Palace (1711–1714), and the first design of the Alexander Nevsky Lavra (monastery) with the Church of the Annunciation (1717–1722). Other notable structures include the Kunstkammer (1718–1734), by Georg Mattarnovy, with a central tower after a design by Andreas Schlüter. At this stage Petersburg's architecture owed much to the northern European Baroque, particularly in Sweden and Holland. The stuccoed brick walls of the city's baroque buildings were painted, with white trim for window surrounds and other details.

Bartolomeo Francesco Rastrelli (1700–1771) defined the high Baroque style during the reigns of Anne and Elizabeth. Among his major projects are Elizabeth's Summer Palace (1741–1743; not extant), the Stroganov Palace (1752–1754), the final version of the Winter Palace (1754–1764), and the Smolny Convent with its Resurrection Cathedral (1748–1764). In addition Rastrelli greatly enlarged the existing Imperial palaces at Peterhof (1746–1752) and Tsarskoe Selo (1748–1756). During this period Russian architects such as Mikhail Zemtsov (1688–1743) and Savva Chevakinsky (1713–1780) contributed significantly to the city's development. Chevakinsky's masterpiece, the Cathedral of St. Nicholas (1753–1762), rivals the best work of Rastrelli.

In the transition from the Baroque to Neoclassicism, favored by Catherine II, Jean-Baptiste Vallin de la Mothe (1729–1800) played a central role with his designs for the Academy of Arts (1764–1788; in collaboration with Aleksandr Filippovich Kokorinov, 1726–1772), the Small Hermitage (1764–1775), the New Holland Arch (1765–1780s), and the arcaded trading center Gostinny Dvor (1757–1785). With the support of Catherine, a constellation of architects endowed the city during the second half of the eighteenth century with a grandeur inspired by classical Rome and Palladianism: Antonio Rinaldi (c.1710–1794) built the Marble Palace (1768–1785) for Catherine's favorite, Grigory Orlov; and Giacomo Quarenghi (1744–1817) designed the Hermitage Theater (1783–1787), the Academy of Sciences (1783–1789), the Smolny Institute for Noblewomen (1806–1808) as well as the Alexander Palace at Tsarskoe Selo (1792–1796). Georg Friedrich Veldten (1730–1801), builder of the Chesme palace and Church of John the Baptist (1777–1780) in the pseudo-Gothic style, enlarged the Hermitage complex and enhanced the beauty of the city with quays along the left bank of the Neva.

Charles Cameron (c.1740–1812), the leading proponent of Palladian architecture in Russia, designed the palace at the imperial estate of Pavlovsk (1780–1796), a gift from Catherine to Grand Duke Paul. Cameron also designed the exquisite pavilions in the Pavlovsk estate park, such as the Temple of Friendship (1780–1782). At Tsarskoe Selo he reconstructed in the manner of Robert Adam and Clerisseau a number of rooms in Rastrelli's Catherine Palace, and attached the Cameron Gallery (1783–1786), with connecting pavilions, to the south wing of the palace. Palace construction in the city continued with Emperor Paul's Mikhailovsky Castle (1797–1800), an Italianate design by Vincenza Brenna and possibly Vasily Bazhenov.

Other major architects of late eighteenth-century Petersburg include Ivan Starov (1745–1808), whose understated classicism in the design of the Tauride Palace (1783–1789) was widely adopted as a model for estate houses. After many delays, Starov completed the central ensemble of the Alexander Nevsky Lavra with his imposing Roman-style Trinity Cathedral (1776–1790). Andrey Voronikhin (1759–1814) created a still more obvious example of the Roman influence in his Cathedral of the Kazan Mother of God (1801–1811), with its sweeping colonnade attached to the north (Nevsky Prospekt) facade. Voronikhin also designed the Mining Institute (1806–1811), whose Doric portico exemplifies the revival of interest in archaic Greek architecture. Similarly, Jean Thomas de Thomon (1760–1813) used the temples at Paestum as a model for the Bourse, or Stock Exchange (1805–1810), on the tip of Vasilevsky Island.

The construction and site plan of the Bourse provided a focus to one of the city's major strategic points, and thus initiated the campaign of Tsar Alexander (1801–1825) to provide an interconnecting system of architectural ensembles and public space throughout the center of Petersburg. The rebuilding of the Admiralty (1806–1823) by Andreian Zakharov (1761–1811) reaffirmed that structure and its spire as dominant elements in the city plan. The culmination of the imperial design fell to Carlo Rossi (1776–1849) who created four major ensembles: the Mikhailovsky Palace and Park (1819–1825); the General Staff Building and Arch

(1819–1829), facing Palace Square; the Alexandrine Theater and adjacent buildings (1828–1832); and the Senate and Holy Synod (1829–1834) facing Senate Square, the site of Etienne Falconet's monument to Peter I ("The Bronze Horseman"; 1768–1782). Vasily Stasov (1769–1848), Petersburg's other master of late Neoclassicism, built a number of churches, including the Icon of the Savior (1817–1823), with the attached building of the Court Stables extending on either side along the Moika Canal.

Neoclassicism in Moscow appeared primarily in houses and other institutions built by the nobility and wealthy merchants. Talented serf architects built many of the grand estate houses, but the most prominent designers of mansions and churches in Moscow were Matvey Kazakov (1738–1812), Rodion Kazakov (1755–1803), and Vasily Bazhenov (1737–1799). Bazhenov also designed, at the request of Catherine II, a grandiose plan for rebuilding the Kremlin in the Neoclassical style. During Catherine's reign, period styles such as pseudo-Gothic had appeared in the work of Bazhenov, and Matvey Kazakov. In the 1770s–1880s Bazhenov and Kazakov were involved in the building of a "Moorish" pseudo-Gothic imperial estate at Tsaritsyno, near Moscow, but Catherine II abandoned the project.

After the fire of 1812, damaged structures such as the Bazhenov's Pashkov House and Kazakov's Moscow University were rebuilt, while new houses appeared in the Empire style as interpreted by Domenico Gilardi (1788–1845), Osip Bove (1784–1834), and Afanasy Grigoriev (1782–1868). In the latter part of the eighteenth century and the early decades of the nineteenth, Neoclassicism spread throughout the provinces, with particularly impressive results in Kaluga and Kostroma.

During the reign of Nicholas I, classical unity in Petersburg yielded to eclecticism and innovations in construction engineering, both of which are evident in the final version of St. Isaac's Cathedral (1818–1858) by Auguste Montferrand (1786–1858) and in mid-nineteenth century palaces by Andrey Shtakenshneider (1802–1865). Mikhail Bykovsky's (1801–1885) design for the estate of Marfino (1831–1845) demonstrated the enduring appeal of the Gothic revival. More significant was the Russo-Byzantine style, supported by Nicholas I and implemented by Konstantin Ton (1794–1881), builder of the Great Kremlin Palace (1838–1849). The major work in this style, which prevailed in church architecture throughout the century, was Ton's Church of Christ the Redeemer (1837–1883; destroyed in 1931), built in Moscow as a memorial to Russian valor in the 1812 war.

Secular architecture in Petersburg and Moscow during the mid-nineteenth century was largely an eclectic combination of various periods in the history of Western architecture. In Petersburg and Moscow applied eclectic decorative styles profusely to the facades of new apartment houses and commercial buildings. By the 1870s there arose a new national style based on decorative elements from sixteenth and seventeenth-century Muscovy as well as on motifs from folk art and traditional wooden architecture. Among the early proponents of this Russian revival style were Ivan Pavlovich Ropet (pseudonym of Ivan Petrov; 1844–1908) and Viktor Hartmann (1834–1873), both of whom played an important role in the early 1870s within the artists' community at Savva Mamontov's Abramtsevo estate. The most significant architectural monument at Abramtsevo is the small Church of the

Icon of the Savior (1881–1882), whose design by the painter Viktor Vasnetsov (1848–1926) incorporated motifs from early medieval Russian architecture.

Major examples of the Russian style in Moscow include the Historical Museum (1874–1883), built on the north side of Red Square to a design by Vladimir Shervud (1833–1897), and the Upper Trading Rows (1889–1893) by Aleksandr Pomerantsev (1848–1918), assisted by the construction engineer Vladimir Shukhov (1853–1939). In Petersburg the Russian style was used by Alfred Parland (1845–92) for the Church of the Resurrection of the Savior "on the Blood" (1883–1907). In Moscow a number of mansions were built in the national style, and its influence continued through the early 1900s as the "neo-Russian" component of the *style moderne*. Painters such as Viktor Vasnetsov, who created the entrance building at the Tretiakov Gallery (ca. 1905), and Sergei Maliutin (1859–1937) were particularly active in using traditional Russian decorative arts as part of a new architectural aesthetic.

The "new style," or *style moderne*, that arose in Russian architecture at the turn of the century included a number of stylistic tendencies. Its main emphasis was on the innovative use of materials such as glass, iron, and glazed brick in functional yet highly aesthetic designs. The style flourished above all in Moscow, where its leading practitioner was Fedor Shekhtel (1859–1926). Shekhtel worked primarily for patrons among Moscow's entrepreneurial elite, such as the Riabushinskys. His most brilliant work was a mansion for Stepan Pavlovich Riabushinsky (1900–1902), although it is rivaled by the more modernist design of the Aleksandr Derozhinskaia mansion (1901). Shekhtel also excelled in the design of commercial buildings. Other leading modernist architects of the period In Moscow include Lev Kekushev (1863–1919), Adolf Erikhson, and William Walcot (1874–1943). All three were involved in the prolonged construction of one of the largest and most significant *moderne* buildings in Russia: the Hotel Metropole (1899–1905). Like Shekhtel, both Kekushev and Walcot produced major examples of the modern style in the design of private houses for wealthy clients.

In Petersburg the *style moderne* appeared primarily in the design of apartment complexes by architects. (Petersburg's relatively compact urban plan impeded the construction of detached private houses.) Yet despite the rapid expansion of apartment space, the lack of adequate housing, particularly for workers, remained a major social problem. The *style moderne* also appeared in Petersburg's commercial buildings such as the Singer Building on Nevsky Prospekt.

By the end of the 1900s, the *style moderne* had yielded to, or merged with, a more severe form of stripped classicism, known in Russia as *neoklassitsizm*. Architects in Petersburg were especially receptive to the neoclassical revival, and they applied it to almost every major structural type, including banks, department stores, apartment buildings, and private houses. One of the most accomplished and versatile architects in this style was, again, Lidval, designer of the Hotel Astoria (1911–12).

In Moscow the most accomplished revivalist was Roman Klein (1858–1924), architect of the Museum of Fine Arts (1897–1912) and the Muir and Mirrielees department store (1906–1908). Although less prolific than Klein, other architects distinguished themselves in a more austere variant of the neoclassical revival for major office buildings in Moscow's commercial center. In contrast to their American contemporaries, Russian architects made little use of the skeletal frame in the design of large buildings, but they applied the techniques of reinforced concrete construction with considerable proficiency.

SOVIET ARCHITECTURE AND BEYOND

The economic chaos engendered in Russia by the First World War proved catastrophic for building activity, and the ensuing revolution and civil war brought architecture to a standstill. With the recovery of the economy in the 1920s, bold new designs—often utopian in concept—brought Russia to the attention of modern architects throughout the world. The theoretical debates and factional disputes of this period are topics for a separate entry. Constructivism, the most productive modernist movement, included architects such as Moisei Ginzburg (1892–1946), Ilia Golosov (1883–1945), Grigory Barkhin (1880–1969), and the Vesnin brothers: Leonid 1880–1933), Viktor (1882–1950), and Aleksandr (1883–1959). Their designs, primarily in Moscow, set a standard for functional design in administrative and apartment buildings, as well as social institutions such as workers' clubs. Another modernist active during the same period, but not a part of Constructivism, was Konstantin Melnikov (1890–1974), known for his designs for exposition pavilions and workers' clubs.

During the 1930s more conservative trends asserted themselves, as designs inspired by classical, Renaissance, and historical models received the party's approval. Prominent traditionalists, much of whose work resembles stripped classicism, included Ivan Zholtovsky (1867–1959), Aleksei Shchusev (1873–1949), and Noi Trotsky (1895–1940). It should be noted that the major traditionalists as well as the modernists had received their training before 1917. After the Second World War, architectural design became still more firmly locked in traditional, often highly ornate eclectic styles, epitomized by the post-war skyscrapers in Moscow and other Soviet cities. Pressing social needs, particularly in housing, led after 1953 to a return to functionalism, heavily dependent on standardized designs and prefabricated components. With the demise of the Communist system in Russia, the revival of private practice in architecture seems likely to change the face of the profession, even as new problems arise in zoning, housing, and resource allocation.

SUGGESTIONS FOR FURTHER READING:

The most comprehensive study in English is William Craft Brumfield, *A History of Russian Architecture* (Cambridge and New York, 1993), with an extensive bibliography. On pre-Mongol architecture, see: Hubert Faensen and Vladimir Ivanov, *Early Russian Architecture* (London, 1971); and Pavel Rappoport, *Building the Churches of Kievan Russia* (Aldershot, Great Britain, 1995).

On later developments, see: Albert Schmidt, *The Architecture and Planning of Classical Moscow* (Philadelphia, 1989); George Heard Hamilton, *The Art and Architecture of Russia* (Baltimore, 1975); Priscilla Roosevelt, *Life on the Russian Country Estate* (New Haven, 1995); William Brumfield, *The Origins of Modernism in Russian Architecture* (Berkeley, 1991); William Brumfield, ed., *Reshaping Russian Architecture: Western technology, utopian dreams* (Cambridge and New York, 1990) [includes material on Russian perceptions of American architecture before 1917];

Selim O. Khan-Magomedov, *Pioneers of Soviet Architecture* (New York, 1987); S. Prederick Starr, *Melnikov: Solo Architect in a Mass Society* (Princeton, 1978); Anatole Kopp, *Town and Revolution: Soviet Architecture and City Planning* (New York, 1970); Alexander Ryabushin and Nadia Smolina, *Landmarks of Soviet Architecture. 1917–1991* (New York, 1992); and William Brumfield and Blair Ruble, eds., *Russian Housing in the Modern Age: Design and Social History* (Cambridge and New York, 1993).

On wooden architecture, see David Buxton, *The Wooden Churches of Eastern Europe: An Introductory Survey* (Cambridge, 1981), and Alexander Opolovnikov, *The Wooden Architecture of Russia* (New York, 1989). On the architecture of the central Russian provinces, see William Brumfield, *Lost Russia: Photographing the Ruins of Russian Architecture* (Durham, 1995). A recommended encyclopedic survey of Russian history and culture is *The Cambridge Encyclopedia of Russia and the Former Soviet Union* (Cambridge, 1994).

An excellent source for English-language maps of Moscow and St. Petersburg, with references to architectural monuments, is R. I. S. Publications (Montpelier, Vermont).

2. RUSSIAN WOODEN ARCHITECTURE

From extensive archaeological and historical data it is evident that wood was used for almost every type of structure in Russia until well into the eighteenth century. By virtue of their settlement within a vast forested zone, Russians were aware of the strength of wood, which they used for every building purpose, from churches and dwellings to fortifications. Fire and decay, however, have long since destroyed the work of early medieval Russian carpenters. The oldest examples of Russian wooden architecture are churches, which were used more carefully than houses, and which could last for centuries, provided rotting logs were promptly replaced and the roof properly maintained. Indeed, the earliest known log building is the Church of the Resurrection of Lazarus, tentatively dated to the late fourteenth century and now preserved on Kizhi Island in Lake Onega. However, extant log structures earlier than the eighteenth century are very rare in Russia.

The simplest type of wooden church—here illustrated by the Church of the Deposition of the Robe (1485) near Ferapontov Monastery on Lake Borodavo and the Church of the Dormition from the village of Nikulino (1599; near Novgorod)—resembles the basic unit of the peasant house, with its pitched roof and rectangular structure. The plan is linear, along an east-west axis, with one part for the service and another, the *trapeza*, as a vestibule. Such churches often have two additional components: an apse containing the altar on the east, and a bell tower attached to the west end of the vestibule, as illustrated in the Church of St. Nicholas from the village of Potakino (1776; near Suzdal) and the Archangel Michael Chapel (eighteenth century, near Kizhi).

The more elaborate churches of this type were decorated with carved end boards that protected the ends of the roof beams, and with carved galleries on raised porches. The variations on this form are many, and include churches with multiple roof constructions to better protect the walls from moisture, as in the Church of St. Nicholas from Tukholia (seventeenth century; near Novgorod). Still more complex variants possessed gables with extensive carving, such as the Church of St. Nicholas from Miakishevo (late seventeenth century; near

9

Kizhi   Church of the Resurrection of Lazarus. Late fourteenth century(?) Southwest view

Borodavo   Church of the Deposition of the Robe. 1485. Southeast view.

Novgorod   Church of the Dormition from the village of Nikulino. 1599. Southeast view.

Novgorod). Some churches of this plan, such as the Transfiguration from the village of Spas-Vezhi (1628; near Kostroma) had very steeply pitched roofs.

Another type of wooden church—the "tent," or *shatior*, so named for the shape of its central tower—emphasized the vertical ascent. The linear arrangement is here replaced with a centralized plan, whose cuboid core supports an octahedron leading to an eight-sided tower, as in Church of the Dormition from the St. Alexander Kushtsky Monastery (ca. 1520; now preserved at the Savior-Prilutsky Monastery, near Vologda) and the Church of the Dormition from Kuritsko (1595; near Novgorod). There were more complex variations which developed a cruciform plan with flanking domes, such as the Church of the Nativity of the Virgin at Peredki (near Novgorod), a monastic structure first mentioned in 1539. The Peredki church is notable for its gallery on three sides, raised above the highest snow drifts on a system of projecting logs (*pomochi*). Although the bulk of the church (approximately 30 meters in height) is austerely monumental, details such as the gallery remind how closely aesthetics and function were combined in log churches.

The Russian love of verticality in church design found expression in a third type of log church, the tiered, or *yarusnyi*, structure, in which a pyramidal silhouette ascends in a series of diminishing octahedrons, as in the Church of the Transfiguration from Kozliatevo (1756; near Suzdal). In some cases the tower is set within a linear plan, as illustrated in the Church of St. Nicholas at Vysoky Ostrov (1757; near Novgorod).

WILLIAM BRUMFIELD

Suzdal   Church of St. Nicholas, from Potakino. 1776. Southwest view.

Kizhi   Archangel Michael Chapel. Late eighteenth century (?) Southwest view.

Novgorod   Church of St. Nicholas from Tukholia. 17th century. Northwest view.

Novgorod   Church of St. Nicholas from Miakishevo. Late 17th century. South view.

In building the churches, the logs were cut in late fall after the final ring of the tree—usually pine, with some fir—had hardened, and they were left on the ground until the beginning of building season, in late spring. The logs were then taken to the construction site, where master carpenters trimmed, notched, and if necessary planed them. The most common tools were the ax (of which there were various types adapted to specific functions) and the adze, as well as wedged spikes for splitting logs and a primitive type of spokeshave, or drawing knife, for making concave incisions along a log. (Russian log structures almost never used

Kostroma   Church of the Transfiguration, from Spas-Vezhi. 1628. Southwest view.

Vologda   Church of the Dormition, Alexander-Kushtsky Monastery. Ca. 1520. East view.

Novgorod Church of the Dormition, from Kuritsko. 1595. Southwest view.

Novgorod   Church of the Nativity of the Virgin, from Peredki. 1539. Southwest view.

Novgorod   Church of the Nativity of the Virgin, from Peredki. Northeast view.

Suzdal Church of the Transfiguration, from Kozliatevo. 1756. Southwest view.

Torzhok   Church of the Ascension. Mid-seventeenth century. Southwest view.

Novgorod   Church of St. Nicholas, from Vysoky Ostrov. 1757. Southeast view.

clay caulking, but relied instead on the tight fit of one log above another, with materials such as moss or hemp for insulation in dwellings.) There was little use for saws, which would have opened the grain of the wood to moisture, as opposed to the proper stroke of the ax, which closed the grain. Nails were also traditionally dispensed with, even in the roof, whose planks—usually double-layered—were designed with a groove fit and wedged at the top into a ridge beam.

The two basic methods of joining the logs were: the notch for round logs, and the mortise and tenon for both round and squared logs. The latter was used when greater precision of detail and stability were required. The logs just beneath the roof were usually extended in length, so as to support an overhang for protection against moisture runoff. The roof planks often had carved tips, which in sunlight cast a pattern of shadows against the log walls. If the church culminated in a tent tower, the base of the tower would be surrounded by an overhang. Such towers were usually planked, but in some instances they were covered with carved shingles, as were the cupolas. These shingles (*lemekhi* or *cheshui*—"fish scales"), among the most ingenious features of Russian wooden architecture, were curved and wedged to follow the contours of the cupola frame. Typically the shingles were carved from moist aspen, which ages from a golden hue to silver, and forms a brilliant contrast to the dark logs of the structure.

The supreme example of these time-honored methods of construction is the tiered Church of the Transfiguration of the Savior on Kizhi Island (the northwest

Kizhi Church of the Transfiguration. 1714. Northwest view, with bell tower (1874) and Church of the Intercession (right background).

Kizhi   Church of the Transfiguration. 1714. South view

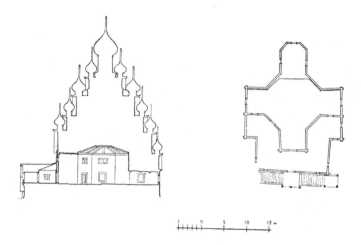

Church of the Transfiguration at Kizhi. Section, plan.

part of Lake Onega), built in 1714. Located on open space in the southwest part of the island, the church formed the center of a *pogost*, a term which by the eighteenth century had come to mean an enclosed cemetery with a parish or district church. Its high pyramidal silhouette (37 meters) signified from a great distance consecrated ground, and the design of the structure reinforces at every point that symbolic purpose. The core is an octahedron in three tiers, buttressed on the lowest—and largest—tier by rectangular extensions at the four compass points. These extensions are also stepped, and thus each of the four provides two additional gables surmounted by a cupolas. The final octagonal tier supports the largest cupola, and the twenty-second cupola rests over a small apse extending from the east. The natural properties of materials are exploited for aesthetic effect in the contrast between the dark walls of aged pine logs and the brilliant silver of the cupolas, covered with a total of some 30,000 curved aspen shingles with stepped points. This elaborate superstructure provided a system of ventilation to preserve the structure from rot; yet the superstructure was not visible from the interior, which was capped at a low level by a painted ceiling, or "sky," over the central part of the church. Apart from the icon screen, the interior walls were unpainted—also typical of Russian log churches. The Church of the Transfiguration was used only during the summer. It was not uncommon in Russian settlements to have paired churches, for summer and winter. At the Kizhi pogost, the adjoining "winter" Church of the Intercession, built in 1764, provides a visual complement to the ensemble by accentuating the horizontal with an extended vestibule.

Although churches comprise the most distinctive examples of Russian log architecture, log dwellings could also display both artistry and the economy of function. The center of the peasant log house was typically a large masonry stove used not only for cooking but also for heating the main living space during the long winters. The stove could be ventilated in two ways that define the basic types of peasant house: the "white" and the "black." In the former the smoke was

Kizhi Church of the Intercession. 1764. South view.

Kizhi   Church of the Intercession. 1764. Detail

released through a brick chimney, while in the latter the smoke drifted up toward the ceiling and a wooden duct that collected the smoke and expelled it. This "black" variant was the more common; and due to the ingenuity of the design, the smoke did not foul the room, but only an area under the roof that could be scraped down.

In the central part of Russia, the house typically formed the main component of a *dvor*, or yard enclosed by a solid fence and containing various sheds for animals, produce, and farm implements. Farther north, the rigors of the climate produced more extensive structures that combined dwelling space with storage sheds and shelter for livestock, all under one roof. The ingenuity required to design and build such houses is still on display in the Vologda area and on Kizhi Island.

Whether large or small, log houses were traditionally decorated with window surrounds and end boards. In the eighteenth and nineteenth centuries, patterns derived from folk motifs became particularly elaborate; yet during the same period, carpenters began to adapt urban architectural motifs such as baroque window surrounds that they might have observed during seasonal work in the cities. As a result vernacular architecture in the Russian provinces during the nineteenth century displayed a rich variety based on tradition and the adaptation of new motifs.

Kostroma Log house. Late nineteenth century.

Novgorod Tsareva house, from Pyrishchi. Early nineteenth century.

Vologda   Popov house, from Vnukovo. Late nineteenth century.

Kizhi   Yakovlev house, from Kleshcheila. 1880s

Kizhi Yakovlev house, from Kleshcheila. Interior, front room.

Kizhi Sergin house, from Monozero. 1880s

3. EARLY MEDIEVAL KIEV

THE CATHEDRAL OF ST. SOPHIA (DIVINE WISDOM). KIEV

There has been much debate about the beginning date of the cathedral's construction, but it is generally accepted that work began in 1037 on the order of grand prince Yaroslav of Kiev. Although the exterior of the cathedral has been modified by reconstruction in the seventeenth and eighteenth centuries (it had fallen into ruin after the Mongol invasion in 1240), excavations in the 1930s and the study of possible designs have furnished what is considered a definitive version of the original. In its basic parts, the plan of Kiev's St. Sophia conforms to the cross-domed model. Of the five aisles, each of which has an apse in the east, the central aisle is twice the width of those flanking—the same proportion as that of the transept along the building's north-south axis. The focal point of the exterior is the main cupola, elevated on a high drum over the central crossing and surrounded by twelve cupolas arranged in descending order. The thick *opus mixtum* walls (composed of narrow brick and a mortar of lime and crushed brick) are flanked by two arcaded galleries on the north, south, and west facades, and by choir galleries on the interior. Therefore, the windows of the cupola drums are the main source of natural light for the interior, which is richly decorated with mosaics within the main cupola and apse and with frescoes throughout the rest of the structure.

CATHEDRAL OF THE TRANSFIGURATION OF THE SAVIOR. CHERNIGOV

Commissioned perhaps as early as 1034 by Prince Mstislav of Chernigov (a rival of Yaroslav of Kiev), the cathedral was probably not completed until the 1050s. The plan of the structure appears similar to the earliest known masonry churches in late tenth-century Kiev: cross-domed and three-aisled, with a narthex. The plan of the church is reflected in the delineation of the facade into bays that correspond to the interior structure and vaulting. The central bay of each facade forms an extension of the arms of the inscribed cross, and each of these bays contains the traditional three windows beneath its curved gable, or *zakomara*. The west front had at

Kiev   Cathedral of St. Sophia. Section.

its north corner a tower with stairs leading to the choir gallery over the narthex. The walls, about 1.5 meters thick, are of opus mixtum, marked with brick niches and decorated with patterns such as the meander, which were later covered in stucco. The five domes achieve the pyramidal, vertical emphasis that would become a distinctive feature of the medieval Russian church. Although badly damaged in the aftermath of the Mongol conquest of 1240, the fragments of mosaics, frescoes, and carved marble that decorated the interior in a style derived from Greek masters.

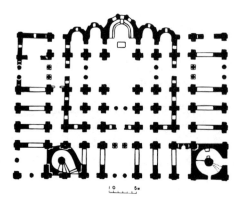

Kiev   Cathedral of St. Sophia. Plan.

Kiev   Cathedral of St. Sophia (Divine Wisdom). 1037(?)–1050s. East view.

Chernigov   Cathedral of the Transfiguration. 1031–1050s. West view.

CATHEDRAL OF SAINTS BORIS AND GLEB. CHERNIGOV

Tentatively dated to the middle of the twelfth century, the cathedral was dedi-cated to the first Russian martyrs, princes Boris and Gleb. Frequently rebuilt, it was restored to its presumed original appearance only after World War II. The simplified plan is typical for masonry churches of this period, with three apses in the east and four bays from east to west. The walls, which are of brick, rather than opus mixtum, were covered with a thin layer of stucco scored to resemble stone. The carved capitals now visible on the attached columns of the exterior are rough copies of the originals, a few of which are on exhibit inside the church. The strap-work carvings on the capitals, as well as other decorative elements, suggest the possibility of western influence, perhaps through connections between ruling families in Kiev and western Europe.

CHURCH OF ST. PARASKEVA PIATNITSA. CHERNIGOV

Dedicated to St. Paraskeva, the patroness of market day (Friday, or *piatnitsa*), this church was built around the turn of the thirteenth century and substantially rebuilt at the end of the seventeenth. After bomb damage in 1943, the church was carefully and reconstructed to what was thought to be its original form. Patterned brickwork decorates the central part of the facades, but the most unusual feature of the small structure is its emphasis on verticality. The single drum and cupola are projected to a height of 24 meters by three corbelled arches, whose massed con-tours provide a visual transition from the upper part of the walls to the cupola.

Chernigov   Cathedral of Saints Boris and Gleb. Mid 12th century. South view.

Chernigov   Church of St. Paraskeva. Early 13th century. West view.

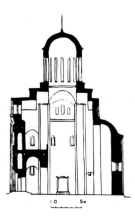

Chernigov   Church of St. Paraskeva. Section.

The recessed portals, outlined with arched brickwork, the blind arcade along the upper part of the apse, the attached profiled columns, and the detailing of the cornice reinforce the aesthetic unity of the structure. The construction technique of the walls consisted of an interior and exterior surface of bricks, with an infill of brick rubble and lime mortar. The piers and vaulting are of solid brick.

4. NOVGOROD: 11TH–14TH CENTURIES

CATHEDRAL OF ST. SOPHIA. NOVGOROD

The oldest surviving and the most imposing monument in the city is the Cathedral of St. Sophia (or Divine Wisdom), built between 1045 and 1050 and located in Novgorod's *detinets*, or citadel, on the west bank of the Volkhov River. The cathedral was commissioned by the prince of Novgorod, Vladimir Yaroslavich, as well as by his father, Yaroslav the Wise (whose own Sophia Cathedral in Kiev was entering its final construction phase), and by Archbishop Luke of Novgorod. With the building of large masonry cathedrals dedicated to the Divine Wisdom in both Kiev and Novgorod, Yaroslav rendered homage to one of the most sacred mysteries of the Orthodox church. Because masonry construction was largely unknown in Novgorod before the middle of the eleventh century, a cathedral of such size and complexity could only have been constructed under the supervision of imported master builders, presumably from Kiev. It is thought that some of the brick was also imported from Kiev. The basic material for the construction of the walls and the piers, however, was obtained in the Novgorod: fieldstone and undressed blocks of limestone set in a mortar of crushed brick and lime. On the exterior, the walls presented a highly textured appearance, even with the spreading of mortar to reduce the unevenness of the surface.

The cathedral has five aisles for the main structure, with enclosed galleries attached to the north, west, and south facades. The north and south galleries each contain chapels on the ground level, and the west gallery includes a round stair tower that leads to the upper levels of all the galleries, including the choir gallery inside the main structure. The Novgorod Sophia is smaller than its Kievan counterpart, yet the two cathedrals are of approximately the same height, and therein lies an explanation for the much sharper sense of vertical development in the Novgorod cathedral. The proportional relation of height to the area of the central structure in the Novgorod cathedral is one and a half times greater than that of Kiev. The emphasis on height is maintained in the interior where the piers of the main aisles soar directly to the barrel vaults without the visual impediment of lowered arches of the type frequently suspended between the piers of St. Sophia in Kiev.

Novgorod   Cathedral of St. Sophia (Divine Wisdom). 1045–52. South view.

Novgorod chronicles indicate that the interior was painted with frescoes over a period of several decades, and fragments of eleventh-century work have been uncovered, as well as early twelfth-century frescoes. Most of the original painting of the interior has long since vanished under centuries of renovations. Although small areas of the interior had mosaic decorations, there were no mosaics comparable to those in Kiev. The exterior facade above the west portal also displays frescoes, but the most distinctive element is the portal itself, with its magnificent

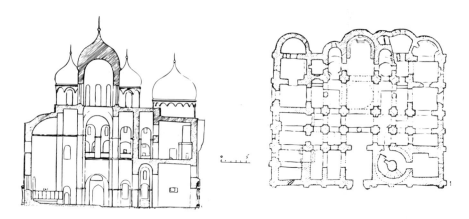

Novgorod   Cathedral of St. Sophia. Section, plan

Novgorod   Cathedral of St. Sophia. East view.

bronze Sigtuna Doors, produced in Magdeburg in the 1050s, and taken from the Varangian fortress of Sigtuna by Novgorod raiders in 1117.

CATHEDRAL OF ST. GEORGE, YUREV MONASTERY. NOVGOROD

The culminating example of early Novgorod's large monastery churches is the Cathedral of St. George, commissioned in 1119 at the Yurev (St. George) Monastery by Prince Vsevolod. According to the chronicles, the builder was a certain Master Peter, one of the few medieval Russian architects whose name has been recorded. On the exterior the vertical development, created by massive pilaster strips that divide the facade into bays, is counterpoised to the horizontality of alternating rows of windows and niches. The restrained detailing of the exterior is directed toward major structural elements: the narrow windows and double-recessed niches complement the rhythm of the facade arches. The walls originally culminated in *zakomary* that followed the contours of the vaulting and provided a visual transition to the three cupolas: the largest over the crossing, the middle over the stair tower, and the smallest situated at the southwest corner. The present domes, in the "helmet" shape, probably replaced smaller domes prevalent in Rus during the 11th and 12th centuries.

On the interior the cruciform piers define the cross-inscribed space, with narthex and attached stair tower on the northwest corner. The walls of St. George's reach a height of 20 meters, and its piers soar to the barrel vaults with no visual impediment. In contrast to the austere monumentality of the facades, the interior was covered with frescoes and contained icons from the prince's workshop—

Novgorod   Cathedral of St. Sophia. Interior

Novgorod   Cathedral of St. George, Yurev Monastery. 1119–30. Southeast view.

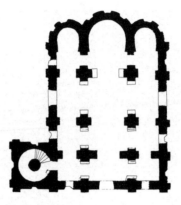

Novgorod   Cathedral of St. George, Yurev Monastery. Plan.

including some of the rarest examples of twelfth-century icon painting. These were most recently repainted at the turn of this century.

CHURCH OF THE NATIVITY OF THE VIRGIN AT ANTONIEV MONASTERY. NOVGOROD

A variation on the endowed monastery church appeared in the Church of the Nativity of the Virgin at Antoniev Monastery (1117–19). Although commissioned by the founder of the monastery, Antony Rimlianin ("the Roman," a convert to Orthodoxy from the West), the church could not have been constructed without the assistance of the Novgorod prince, both for political reasons and because the prince still held a monopoly on the materials and the builders necessary for masonry construction. The Church of the Nativity displays the expected elements of Novgorod church architecture during this period; but it also contains a number of innovative features. The two west piers under the central crossing are octagonal (as opposed to the cruciform piers almost universally used in medieval Russian church architecture), which creates an sense of space in the center of what is a relatively narrow structure. The choir gallery above the narthex is reached by a stair tower attached to the northwest corner of the building, but its shape is round, rather than the usual square extension housing a round stairwell. This form, together with a simplification of exterior details, heightens a sense of the plasticity of the structure, whose walls were in any event more crudely molded than those of the early twelfth-century princely churches.

CHURCH OF ST. THEODORE STRATILATES ON THE BROOK. NOVGOROD

The Church of St. Theodore was commissioned by Semion Andreevich, the *posadnik*, or mayor, of Novgorod, whose generosity made this one of the larger fourteenth-century churches. Its trefoil facade is extended to the west in order to reconcile the basic cuboid plan with the need to provide space for the congregation. The north and south facades each have a recessed portal with a profiled arch.

Novgorod   Cathedral of St. George, Yurev Monastery. Interior.

Novgorod   Cathedral of the Nativity of the Virgin, Antoniev Monstery. 1117–19. East view.

The rhythm of curve and arch appears extensively on the facades and on the drum, whose narrow windows are capped by eyebrow arches and a scalloped-wave cornice beneath the dome. On the interior a high wall separated the west bays of the choir gallery from the main space—a device used in mid-fourteenth-century churches to create additional chapels. There is no documentary evidence for the frescoes, which were whitewashed in the 1870s and subsequently restored in fragments. They appear to date from the late 1370s.

CHURCH OF THE TRANSFIGURATION OF THE SAVIOR ON ELIJAH STREET.

The most significant monument of the Novgorod revival in the mid-fourteenth century, is the Church of the Transfiguration on Elijah Street, built in 1374 for the residents of the major street through one of the city's commercial districts. The plan of the Church of the Transfiguration of the Savior consists of a four-pillared arrangement with the bias to the west, reflected on the exterior panels. On the west facade the church had an enclosed extension and belltower, which were razed (perhaps in the late eighteenth century) and replaced. The later variants have since been removed, and the west facade now shows the arch of the original extension. On the interior the northwest and southwest bays were enclosed as corner chapels. The north chapel was reached by a stairway set within the thickness of the west wall—a common device in medieval brick churches. The central bay in the west is spanned by a wooden passageway leading to the south chapel.

Novgorod   Church of St. Theodore Stratilates on the Brook. 1360–61. Southeast view.

Novgorod Church of the Transfiguration of the Savior on Elijah Street. 1374. Southeast view.

In 1378 the boyar Vasily Danilovich commissioned frescoes for the church from Theophanes the Greek, an experienced artist from Constantinople who had recently arrived in Novgorod. Theophanes—or Feofan, as he was known to the Russians—painted icons as well as frescoes, and the Church of the Transfiguration is his only documented church interior in Novgorod. Despite their fragmentary

Novgorod Church of SS. Peter and Paul in Kozhevniki. 1406. Southeast view.

nature, the frescoes of the church are sufficient to establish his reputation as one of the greatest painters of medieval Russia.

CHURCH OF SAINTS PETER AND PAUL IN KOZHEVNIKI. NOVGOROD

The Church of Saints Peter and Paul in Kozhevniki (1406), displays a number of stylistic refinements in comparison with the Church of the Transfiguration on Elijah Street, which it closely resembles. The decorative patterns are focused on the middle bay—particularly on the west and south facades—rather than distributed over the entire surface. The appearance of new ornamental motifs in brick, such as rosettes and a continuous band of eyebrow arches on the main drum, provides a textural contrast to the main surface of the walls, constructed of a deep-red, rough shellstone that was originally unstuccoed. Brick is also used for the pilaster strips, which delineate the facade, and for the arcaded attached columns on the apse.

Every feature of the exterior of the Church of Sts. Peter and Paul, whether minor or of major structural significance such as the recessed portals, emphasizes the unity of form and plasticity of material characteristic of Novgorodian architecture during the height of its revival in the late fourteenth and early fifteenth centuries. As was often the case, this church underwent substantial modifications in the sixteenth century, including the replacement of the roof and the creation of a second story by building a wooden floor on the level of the choir gallery. After substantial damage in the Second World War, a meticulous restoration supervised by Grigory Shtender stripped the remaining stucco from the facades and re-created the trefoil cornice with its wooden shingled roof.

5. THE VLADIMIR AREA: 11TH–13TH CENTURIES

CATHEDRAL OF THE TRANSFIGURATION. PERESLAVL-ZALESSKY

The Cathedral of the Transfiguration, built by prince Yury Dolgoruky in 1152–57, is one of the earliest preserved examples of a style that would soon lead to an extraordinary series of monuments. Although it lacks the harmony of proportions that characterizes churches built by Yury Dolgoruky's sons, the plan is finely calculated (particularly in the main vaulting arches) and demonstrates the facility with which limestone ashlar was used as the basic structural material. No other area of medieval Rus produced cut stonework of such precision for structural purposes, and the reasons for its sudden appearance in Suzdalia are still unresolved.

The upper bays of the walls are recessed, but the facades are devoid of decoration, except for an ornamental frieze on the apse and drum. Access to the choir gallery presumably occurred through an opening in a bay of the north facade, linked by a wooden passageway to the princely residence—also of wood. (Construction of a passage from the palace to the choir gallery of the main cathedral was not uncommon at that time.) Structural evidence suggests that the original roofing material consisted of wooden shingles. The Cathedral of the Transfiguration provides the basic design for all but one of Suzdalia's major twelfth-century churches: a cross-domed plan, with a triple apse and four piers supporting a single cupola.

THE CHURCH OF THE INTERCESSION ON THE NERL. BOGOLIUBOVO (NEAR VLADIMIR)

Located a short distance from Andrei Bogoliubsky's palace (not extant) at Bogoliubovo, the church honors the festival of the Intercession of the Mother of God, derived from a Byzantine miracle but elevated to a major religious holiday by Andrei. Built within one construction season in 1165 or 1166, the church follows the cross-inscribed design, with four piers, a single dome, and a tripartite facade

Pereslavl-Zalessky   Cathedral of the Transfiguration of the Savior. 1152–57. Northwest view.

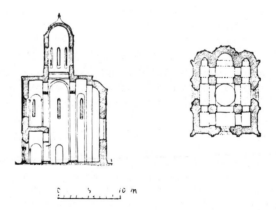

Bogoliubovo   Church of the Intercession on the Nerl. Section, plan.

Bogoliubovo (near Vladimir)   Church of the Intercession of the Virgin on the Nerl. 1165.
West view.

Bogoliubovo   Church of the Intercession on the Nerl. Southeast view.

Bogoliubovo　　Church of the Intercession on the Nerl. Interior.

culminating in *zakomary*. Yet subtle modifications in design create a remarkable sense of proportional harmony. The unknown architect selected a site, on low, marshy ground near the confluence of the Kliazma and Nerl Rivers. On this difficult location, exposed to spring floods as high as four meters, the builders fashioned an artificial hill, paved with stone, that protected the church from high water and provided a buttress for the deep foundation walls (five meters). In its original form the structure appears to have been buttressed by a one-story gallery on the north, west, and south facades. The gallery provided access to the choir gallery through an entryway still visible on the upper level of the south facade.

The structure rises in two tiers: a lower story of thick walls, culminating in an arcade band; and the upper-facade panels, deeply recessed within the three bays of each wall. The vertical thrust is reinforced by the receding surface of the walls, and by a slight calculated lean inward, which creates a foreshortened effect. The perspective arches of the portals define a focal point at the base of the structure, while the rhythm of the arched bays is repeated in the arcade strip and in the narrow stepped windows of the upper tier. The ascent is completed by the drum, whose recessed windows echo those of the walls. (The onion dome is a nineteenth-century distortion.)

The Church of the Intercession is the earliest surviving monument to display an iconographic message in stone. The white limestone provided a durable material suitable for carving, and the rapid development of this form of exterior ornamentation at Andrei's Bogoliubovo churches (both completed by 1165) and the appearance of perspective portals suggests the participation of foreign masters familiar with the Romanesque style in central Europe. The carvings include foliated patterns on the archivolts of the portals and on the capitals of the attached columns, as well as bestial and human figures on the facades. The dominant element in the latter group is a high-relief carving of King David, placed in each of the central *zakomary*. The prominence allotted David suggests various interpretations: as God's anointed, the king of Judah, he represents the warrior-leader who defeated his enemies and united the various factions within his kingdom—deeds Andrei would have compared to his own frequent campaigns.

More precisely, however, the name of the church honors the intercession of the Virgin, whose protection is extended to the people of Vladimir and their ruler. No representation of Mary appears on the Church of the Intercession, but the concept of feminine protection is expressed in the twenty high-relief masks of braided maidens, placed sightly below the *zakomary*. Striking in their stylized primitive form, the masks suggest not only the exaltation of the feminine in Orthodox religious art, but also the celebration of fertility and the reverence for the Russian earth.

CATHEDRAL OF THE DORMITION. VLADIMIR

The first church commissioned by Andrei Bogoliubsky in Vladimir itself, the Cathedral of the Dormition (1158–60), conformed to the elongated, six-pier plan typical of large churches in Kiev and Novgorod during the same period, Among the distinctive features of the limestone structure were a large drum and cupola, with twelve windows and 24 columns with carved capitals. After a fire that destroyed much of Vladimir, Prince Vsevolod III (half-brother of Andrei Bogoliubsky) ordered the rebuilding of the severely damaged Dormition Cathedral in 1185. Vsevolod's builders retained the walls of the earlier structure, weakened by fire, as the core of the cathedral, and added another aisle on each side. The bays of the now interior walls were widened to create piers (bolstered by

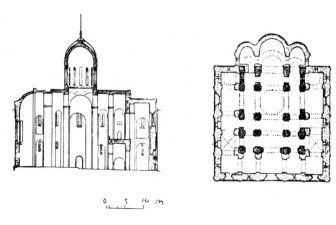

Vladimir   Dormition Cathedral. Section, plan.

Vladimir   Cathedral of the Dormition. 1158–60; 1185–89. Southwest view.

Vladimir   Cathedral of the Dormition. East view

pylons), and the choir gallery was extended over cross vaults to the west aisle. On the east the apsidal structure was completely rebuilt, with a substantial increase in depth. On the other facades, the new walls were raised two stories, but not to the full height of the original structure. The relation between the old and the new was thus clearly defined in the structure.

The exterior walls are marked at mid-level by an arcade frieze but relatively little carved ornament. The walls themselves possess a sculpted quality, with the recessed upper bays delineated by attached columns, and the festive row of *zakomary* outlined in decorative metalwork. The most noticeable change in the design of the new cathedral consisted of four additional cupolas, placed over bays to the north and south of the corners of the original structure. As before, the walls of the drums were sheathed in gilded copper; and although the basic roofing material was sheet lead, there is evidence that the large central cupola was also covered with gilded copper. The rebuilding of the Cathedral of the Dormition produced one of the largest masonry structures in medieval Rus. As the center of religious authority in the large domains of Suzdalia, the cathedral also represented a monument to Vsevolod's power and to the cultural renaissance that it fostered.

CATHEDRAL OF ST. DMITRY. VLADIMIR

Soon after the rebuilding of the Dormition Cathedral, Vsevolod commissioned for his own use a church dedicated to St. Demetrius of Salonika. Built between 1193 and 1197, the church is similar in plan to the cuboid structure of the Bogoliubovo churches, with an arcade frieze separating two tiers, the upper of which is covered in carved limestone. Although Vsevolod's sculptors undoubtedly drew on motifs and techniques developed three decades earlier at Bogoliubovo, there is no clear source for the extraordinary iconographic exercise of the facades of the Cathedral of St. Dmitry. The Romanesque elements introduced in Bogoliubsky's churches are still in evidence, but some have argued in favor of borrowings from Balkan churches or from the carved tufa facades of Armenian churches. No precise evidence exists for any one theory of derivation, and in view of the transience of

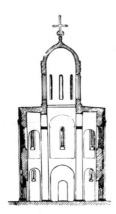
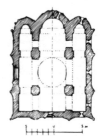

Vladimir   Cathedral of St. Dmitry. Section, plan.

Vladimir   Cathedral of St. Dmitry. 1193–97. Southwest view.

Vladimir   Cathedral of St. Dmitry. West facade, central bay.

motifs and craftsmen—from Byzantium, the Balkans, central Europe, and, possibly, the Caucasus—it is likely that Vsevolod's artisans adapted and combined elements from several sources.

Furthermore, there is the iconographic question posed by the carvings, whose
order has been partially preserved despite reconstruction and renovation over a
period of eight centuries—the most extensive being a restoration begun in 1832.
The original carvings on the exterior display a system of religious, secular, and
ornamental motifs that comprise a message in stone. Although the fanciful plant
and animal carvings appear to have a primarily decorative function, the human figures have in many cases been identified, and it is possible to read the facades as a
text on the prince whose authority is sanctioned by God, by the Orthodox Church
and its saints, and by legendary rulers of antiquity. The military component, so
essential to the maintenance of princely power, is emphasized not only in references to Alexander the Great and King David, but also to "warrior saints." The
Russian saints Boris and Gleb also appear on the arcade frieze of the north facade.

As at the Church of the Intercession on the Nerl, King David dominates the central *zakomara* of the west facade. The same position on the south facade contains
Solomon, law-giver, poet, and builder of the Temple. Surrounding David are creatures of the sky and the earth, among them eagles, doves, peacocks, lions, pan-
thers, pheasants, hares, as well as fantastic creatures such as griffins, centaurs, and
the basilisk. As representations of the wise and strong ruler, David and Solomon

Vladimir Cathedral of St. Dmitry. South portal. Carved ornament.

Vladimir Cathedral of St. Dmitry. North facade

are complemented by mythological and historical figures such as Hercules and Alexander the Great. The emphasis on great rulers seems to overshadow the image of Christ, but in symbolic terms, all of the rulers and mythological figures would have been interpreted as part of an elaborate system of commentary on the majesty of Christ.

On the interior, carved details such as crouching lions on impost blocks are preserved, but most of the frescoes have been destroyed. The central and south vaults beneath the choir gallery still display a remarkable set of frescoes, probably painted around 1195, on the theme of the Last Judgement. The predominant scholarly opinion now assigns the major part of this work to a master from Constantinople, with frescoes by Russian assistants in the south vault. Vsevolod's mother was a Byzantine princess, Vsevolod himself spent seven years of his youth in the city, and his brother Mikhail established in Vladimir a school with Greek clerics and a library with extensive holdings of Greek manuscripts. Although the library is long destroyed, its manuscripts were a possible source for the iconographic motifs of Vsevolod's church.

CATHEDRAL OF THE NATIVITY OF THE MOTHER OF GOD. SUZDAL

An earlier church on the site, constructed around 1102 by Vladimir Monomachus, had already undergone a number of major repairs. At the command of Prince Yury, son of Vsevolod III, the structure was rebuilt in 1222–25 primarily of a light tufa, with limestone for the details. Rubble from the plinthos walls of the Monomachus church was used for the core infill. In 1445 the cathedral collapsed. When rebuilt in 1528–1530, the remaining stone walls were lowered to the level of the arcade frieze, while the upper structure and drums were rebuilt of new brick in the pentacupolar style of large Muscovite churches.

This cathedral shows substantial differences with earlier limestone churches in the area, in both plan and detail. The main bay of each facade contains an enclosed extension with portal, and the arcade strip is here recessed into the wall surface, thus assuming a purely decorative role. The surface iconography is limited to female masks (indicative of the dedication of the cathedral) placed on the pilaster strips, with heraldic lions at the corners and on certain of the capitals of the attached columns framing the portals. The primary iconographic setting of the cathedral was transferred from the structural surface to the "Golden Doors" of the west portal, tentatively dated 1233, and to a later pair in the south portal (ca. 1248). The scenes portrayed in the panels of both sets of doors were executed by applying gold foil to copper plate; and although the combination of Biblical scenes, Byzantine theologians and saints venerated in Rus, and heraldic beasts can yield ingenious religious and political interpretations, the setting of the doors and the artistic medium create a miniaturization of the iconographic message.

CATHEDRAL OF ST. GEORGE. YUREV-POLSKOI

The tendency toward ornamentalism in the limestone churches of the Vladimir area culminates in the limestone cathedral constructed in Yurev-Polskoi by Sviatoslav, another of the sons of Vsevolod. Founded by Yury Dolgoruky in the

Suzdal Cathedral of the Nativity of the Virgin. 1222–25. Southwest view.

Suzdal   Cathedral of the Nativity of the Virgin. South facade. Portal detail.

middle of the twelfth century, the town had been included in the Vladimir principality; but with the distribution of lands among Vsevolod's sons in 1212, it became the seat of a small principality under Sviatoslav. In 1230 he commissioned a rebuilding of Dolgoruky's Church of St. George (1152), and by 1234 the new cathedral was completed. When the upper part of the church collapsed in the 1460s, Ivan III, grand prince of Moscow, commanded the architect Vasily Ermolin to rebuild the structure as part of a campaign to restore the lustre of the ancient centers of Suzdalia, now absorbed into Muscovy .

In 1471 Ermolin completed his task, but with scant concern for the original appearance. Perhaps there was little choice, since the original design, which seems to have daringly elevated the large drum and cupola above the main walls, may

Yurev-Polskoi   Cathedral of St. George. 1230–34. South facade

Yurev-Polskoi   Cathedral of St. George. South facade. Detail.

have been unstable. Furthermore, the intricate patterned carving that covered the facades could hardly have been recreated in the absence of a concern for scholarly accuracy in such matters. Many of the carved blocks were restored to the new walls in whatever fashion, yet a number were used for the vaulting, or for other hidden structural purposes. Much of the extant surface, therefore, is chaotic, with the exception of the relatively intact north wall.

Although considerably smaller that the Nativity Cathedral in Suzdal, the Cathedral of St. George is similar in its three extensions for the portals of the north, west, and south facades. As at Suzdal the west extension is much larger: two stories, with an upper level replacing the usual choir gallery within the main structure. Because it lacked a choir gallery, the interior of this four-piered church was unusually spacious and well illuminated by two tiers of unobstructed windows. The interior walls would have had the usual complement of frescoes, but the more striking iconographic display remained on the exterior. It is thought that the Cathedral of St. George was built to celebrate a major victory of Sviatoslav's forces over the Volga Bulgars in 1220, and consequently the biblical scenes, saints, and church fathers that appear in relief carving signify the divine protection extended to the prince and his people. In addition the surface was covered with a low relief vegetal pattern carved when the blocks were already in place. The dense ornament covered all of the lower structure, including the attached columns.

6. MEDIEVAL MUSCOVY: 15TH–16TH CENTURIES

CATHEDRAL OF THE NATIVITY OF THE VIRGIN AT SAVVA-STOROZHEVSKY MONASTERY AND CATHEDRAL OF THE DORMITION. ZVENIGOROD

The first major surviving examples of masonry architecture in Muscovy are situated in the town of Zvenigorod, to the west of Moscow. By the end of the fourteenth century, Prince Yury, son of Moscow's grand prince Dmitry Donskoi, had gathered sufficient resources to found a monastery subsequently known as Savva-Storozhevsky. In addition to the monastery Yury developed the fortified center of Zvenigorod. At the turn of the fifteenth century, he commissioned two stone cathedrals: the Dormition, which served as the court church within the city's fortress, and the Nativity of the Virgin, located in the monastery. Both churches follow the plan of their twelfth-century predecessors at Vladimir and Bogoliubovo, with a central cube containing four piers, which support a single drum and cupola, and with three apses extending from the sanctuary's eastern wall. Each facade is divided into three parts by attached columns, and the portals are framed by perspective arches.

Yet, in comparison with the limestone churches of pre-Mongol Vladimir, Yury's cathedrals display a simplified notion of design, in which the complex relation of structure and ornament characteristic of Vladimir is replaced by a few insistently repeated decorative motifs, such as the profusion of ogival arches between the cornice and the cupola drum of the Nativity Cathedral. The Cathedral of the Dormition, whose pointed arches were removed in a later rebuilding of the roof, bears a greater resemblance to the churches of Andrei Bogoliubsky, with its emphasis on verticality enhanced by a slight tapering of the walls; but the exterior division of the walls no longer corresponds to the interior arrangement of pier and vault. Furthermore, there is no blind arcading, and the carved decorative strips consist of a foliate pattern repeated without variation for the length of the band, instead of the variety of mythological and Biblical subjects of the Vladimir churches.

Zvenigorod   Cathedral of the Dormition. 1399(?). Southeast view.

Zvenigorod   Cathedral of the Nativity of the Virgin, Savva-Storozhevsky Monastery. 1405(?) Northeast view.

TRINITY CATHEDRAL AT TRINITY-ST. SERGIUS MONASTERY. SERGIEV POSAD

The Trinity Cathedral was jointly endowed in 1422 by Prince Yury of Zvenigorod and Grand Prince Vasily I to provide an imposing monument to Sergius of Radonezh (1319?–1392), founder of the monastery and one of the inspiring forces in the development of Russian monastic communities. (St. Sergius was buried under an earlier log version of the church, which burned during a Tartar raid in 1408.) In comparison with the Zvenigorod churches, the Trinity Cathedral seems a step backward: its decoration is more austere (a repetition of the carved ornamental strips along the upper facade and drum), and there is no clear relation between the interior bays and the design of the facade. Only from the east and west perspectives is the structural balance evident, emphasized by the buttressing inward lean of the walls and the cupola drum. Despite the peculiarities of its design, the Trinity Cathedral at the time of its construction would have presented a striking contrast to the rest of the monastery and its surrounding wall—all of logs.

CATHEDRAL OF THE ICON OF THE SAVIOR AT SAVIOR-ANDRONIKOV MONASTERY. MOSCOW

Located within the Savior-Andronikov Monastery (named for its first prior, Andronik, a disciple of St. Sergius), this church is considered the earliest surviving monument in Moscow. At some point between 1410 and 1427 the church was apparently endowed by the Ermolins, a Muscovite merchant family. The structure is the most ornamental to be found in Muscovy at that time. The ascent of pointed *zakomary* and decorative *kokoshniki*, culminating in a high drum and cupola, creates a vertical thrust that is reinforced by a lowering of the corner vaults. It has been suggested that this design, with an octagon of *kokoshniki* serving as a visual transition from the central cube to the drum, is a prototype for Moscow's tower churches of the sixteenth century.

CATHEDRAL OF THE NATIVITY OF THE VIRGIN AT FERAPONTOV MONASTERY. FERAPONTOVO

Although modest in size, the Ferapontov Monastery, located in north Russia near Lake Beloe, is rich both in history and in works of art. Founded in 1398, the monastery experienced sustained development only in the latter part of the fifteenth century. Its first masonry structure, the brick Cathedral of the Nativity of the Virgin, was built in 1490 in a simple cross-inscribed plan (with four piers) typical of the mid-fifteenth century. In 1502 the interior was painted by one of the greatest medieval Russian artists, Dionisy, assisted by his two sons. Perhaps because of the small monastery's remote location, the frescoes are remarkably well preserved. The church itself was frequently modified (particularly its roof gables and cupola), and two other churches were attached to it: the Church of the Annunciation (1530–24, with refectory), whose *kokoshniki* gables have been

Sergiev Posad   Cathedral of the Trinity, Trinity-St. Sergius Monastery. 1422. East view.

Moscow Cathedral of the Icon of the Savior, Savior-Andronikov Monastery. 1410–27(?).
Southwest view.

WILLIAM BRUMFIELD

Moscow   Cathedral of the Icon of the Savior, Savior-Andronikov Monastery. Interior.

Ferapontovo   Cathedral of the Nativity of the Virgin, Ferapontov Monastery. 1490.
Northeast view.

restored; and the Church of St. Martinian (1640), with its tent tower. On the west side, the ensemble is connected by a raised gallery, from which rises a seventeenth-century bell tower.

CATHEDRAL OF THE DORMITION. MOSCOW KREMLIN

The rebuilding of the primary cathedral of Moscow, the Dormition of the Mother of God, began in the early 1470s with the support of Grand Prince Ivan III and Metropolitan Philip, leader of the Russian Orthodox church. Local builders proved incapable of so large and complex a task, and when a portion of the walls collapsed, Ivan obtained the services of an Italian architect and engineer, Aristotle Fioravanti, who arrived in Moscow in 1475. He was instructed to model his structure on the Cathedral of the Dormition in Vladimir; and while his design incorporates certain features of the Russo-Byzantine style (particularly the large central cupola, with lesser cupolas at the corners), the architect also introduced a number of innovations: stout oak piles for the foundation, iron tie rods for the vaulting, and strong bricks (instead of stone) for the vaults and cupola drums. The limestone exterior reflects the perfect proportions of the equilateral bays of the plan, and the interior—with round columns instead of massive piers—is lighter and more spacious than any previous Muscovite church.

MOSCOW KREMLIN WALLS

In the 1460s, the condition of the Kremlin's late fourteenth-century limestone walls had reached a dangerous state of disrepair. Local contractors were hired for patchwork; but for a fundamental reconstruction, Ivan III turned to Italy for specialists in fortification. Between 1485 and 1516, the old fortress was replaced with brick walls and towers extending 2,235 meters and ranging in thickness from 3.5 to 6.5 meters. The height of the walls varied from 8 to 19 meters, with the distinctive Italian "swallowtail" crenellation. Of the twenty towers, the most elaborate were placed on the corners or at the main entrances to the citadel. Among the most imposing is the Frolov (later Spassky, or Savior, Tower), built in 1464–66 by Vasily Ermolin and rebuilt in 1491 by Pietro Antonio Solari, who arrived in Moscow from Milan in 1490. The decorative crown was added in 1624–25 by Bazhen Ogurtsov and the Englishman Christopher Halloway. At the southeast corner of the walls, the Beklemishev Tower (1487–88, with an octagonal spire from 1680) was constructed by Marco Friazin, who frequently worked with Solari. This and similar Kremlin towers suggest comparisons with the fortress at Milan. The distinctive spires, however, were added by local architects in the latter part of the seventeenth century.

FACETED CHAMBERS. MOSCOW KREMLIN

Although he built no cathedrals, Pietro Antonio Solari played a major role in the renovation of the Kremlin not only with his four entrance towers—the Borovitsky, the Constantine and Helen, the Frolov, and the Nikolsky (all 1490–1493)—as well

Moscow Kremlin   Southeast view.

Moscow   Cathedral of the Dormition, Kremlin. 1475–79. Southeast view.

Moscow   Dormition Cathedral. Section.

Moscow   Cathedral of the Dormition. East view.

Moscow Beklemishev Tower, Kremlin. 1490–93. South view, with Savior (Spassky) Tower in background.

Moscow Faceted Chambers, Kremlin. 1487–90s

as the magnificent corner Arsenal Tower and the Kremlin wall facing Red Square, but also for his role in the completion of the "Faceted Chambers" (*Granovitaia palata*), so named for the diamond-pointed rustication of its limestone main facade. Used for banquets and state receptions within the Kremlin palace complex, the building was begun in 1487 by Marco Friazin, who designed the three-storied structure with a great hall whose vaulting was supported by a central pier. A similar plan had been used for the archbishop's palace in Novgorod, but the distinctive feature of the Kremlin structure was its Italianate decoration, thought to have been the work of Solari, who assumed control of the project in 1490.

The main (east) facade of the building is marked at each end by narrow attached columns with a spiral incision and capitals, but also in a monumental entrance porch and stairway on the south facade. (This stairway was reconstructed in 1993.) The original unstuccoed brick side walls were painted a dark red, which provided a dramatic contrast to the limestone front. Much of the ornamental detail, however, was modified or effaced during a rebuilding of the Chambers by Osip Startsev in 1682. The original pairs of narrow windows in a late-Gothic style were replaced by the present wider frames, with elaborate carved columns and entablature; and the steep roof was replaced with one much lower.

CATHEDRAL OF THE ARCHANGEL MICHAEL. MOSCOW KREMLIN

The ensemble of Kremlin cathedrals commissioned by Ivan III concludes with the Cathedral of the Archangel Michael, built in 1505–08 by Aleviz Novy. The building displays the most extravagantly Italianate features of the Kremlin's "Italian Period," and yet it also represents a return to the more traditional forms of large Russian cross-inscribed churches. The "scallop" motif—a Venetian feature soon to enter the repertoire of Moscovy's architects—provides an emphatic accent to the exterior walls, which are divided with an array of cornices, arches, and pilasters. The wall paintings on the interior date from the mid-seventeenth century, and contain in addition to religious subjects the portraits of Russian rulers, including those buried in the cathedral from the sixteenth to the end of the seventeenth centuries.

CATHEDRAL OF THE DORMITION. ROSTOV KREMLIN

The Dormition and Archangel Michael Cathedrals of the Moscow Kremlin represent a revival of the pre-Mongol design of five cupolas over an elongated variant of the cross-inscribed plan. This arrangement of drums and cupolas became a distinctive feature of other large cathedrals, such as the Cathedral of the Dormition in Rostov, built perhaps as early as the late fifteenth century on the site of two earlier limestone versions of the cathedral dating from the twelfth and thirteenth centuries. Whatever the new design of the Rostov Dormition Cathedral derived from its antecedent structures, it was more directly influenced by the design of the Moscow Dormition Cathedral, which in its turn derived much of its exterior detail from the twelfth-century Vladimir Dormition Cathedral. Thus the blind arcade beneath the windows of the second tier of the Rostov cathedral is a feature of Suzdalian architecture reinterpreted in the manner of the fifteenth century. With no

Moscow   Cathedral of Archangel Michael, Kremlin. 1505–08. North view.

Moscow   Cathedral of the Archangel Michael. Plan, section.

Moscow   Cathedral of Archangel Michael. West view.

Rostov Cathedral of the Dormition. Early 16th century. Southwest view.

structural purpose, the arcading displays decorative elaborations (on the column shafts and the pointed arches) characteristic of early fifteenth-century Muscovite churches. Whether it occurred in the reign of Ivan III or of Basil III, the rebuilding of the Rostov cathedral demonstrated Moscow's dominant political position as well as its determination to maintain the ancient centers of Russian culture.

CONVENT OF THE INTERCESSION OF THE MOTHER OF GOD. SUZDAL

The influence of the late 15th-century Kremlin cathedral rapidly spread to monastic structures, such as the Cathedral of the Intercession of the Mother of God at the Intercession, or Pokrovsky, Convent in Suzdal. Built in 1510–1514, during the reign of Basil III, the cuboid brick structure displayed features of early Muscovite churches, such as the pointed *kokoshniki* in an octagonal arrangement at the base of the drum and the ornamental brick and terra cotta motif beneath the main cupola. Yet it also has blind arcading on the facade and a level row of zakomary—devices common in early Suzdalian architecture and revived through Moscow's Dormition Cathedral. The Intercession Cathedral has three cupolas—two over chapels within the eastern corner bays, in the manner of the Kremlin's Annunciation Cathedral—and an exterior gallery. This and other churches in the convent were commissioned as votive churches by Basil III and his first wife, Solomoniia Saburova, in supplication for the birth of an heir. In 1525 an impending dynastic crisis led Basil, with the support of the church, to annul his marriage to Saburova, who then entered this same Suzdal Intercession Convent.

Suzdal   Cathedral, Intercession of the Virgin Convent. 1510–34. Northeast view.

Novgorod   Cathedral of Transfiguration at Khutyn Monastery. 1515. Southeast view.

CATHEDRAL OF THE TRANSFIGURATION AT KHUTYN MONASTERY. NEAR NOVGOROD

The growing influence of Moscow in the architecture of Novgorod during the six-teenth century is particularly evident in large monastery churches in the area sur-rounding Novgorod, such as the Cathedral of the Transfiguration commissioned by Basil III in 1515 at the Khutyn Monastery. Among its Muscovite features are the use of a triple apsidal structure, and the return to a pentacupolar design that had long been abandoned in Novgorod architecture. Currently under restoration by the Orthodox Church, the interior is one of the most majestic examples of brick vaulting in sixteenth-century Russian architecture. Similar Muscovite elements appeared in more modest parish churches such as Sts. Boris and Gleb in Plotniki, built in 1536 by a group of merchants from Moscow and Novgorod.

SAVIOR-PRILUTSKY MONASTERY. VOLOGDA

Established to the northwest of Vologda in 1371, the Savior-Prilutsky Monastery was supported by Moscow's grand prince Dmitry as a bulwark of Orthodox Moscow in the rich but difficult terrain of the northern forests. Its main structure is also the oldest: the Cathedral of the Savior, built in 1537–42 with financial assis-tance from Moscow. Although similar in design to other large monastery churches that derived ultimately from the main Kremlin cathedrals (and thus extended Moscow's power by visual means), this structure is unusually dynamic in form,

Novgorod   Cathedral of Transfiguration at Khutyn Monastery. Interior.

Novgorod   Church of SS Boris and Gleb in Plotniki. 1536

with two rows of curved gables (*zakomary*) leading to a clearly differentiated ensemble of five cupolas. The main cupola, much larger than the flanking four, creates a strong vertical point to the pyramidal shape. A raised gallery attached to the structure on three sides leads on the southeast corner to a refectory and Church of the Presentation, built in the late 1540s. The ensemble is completed by a large bell tower, rebuilt in the mid-seventeenth century. The interior of the Savior Cathedral, whose white-washed walls were never painted with frescoes, displays an monumental austerity, from the four piers to the corbelled vaulting beneath the cupola drums.

CHURCH OF ARCHANGEL MICHAEL ON THE TRADING SIDE. NOVGOROD

The development of more elaborate forms of church architecture throughout Russia in the sixteenth century is reflected in Novgorod in an ensemble created in the middle of the sixteenth century by the rebuilding of two adjacent churches: the Archangel Michael and the Annunciation on the Trading Side. Originally associated with a commercial district, the grouping of churches and bell tower with courtyard gate was restored after the Second World War, with attention to characteristic details such as the use of wooden structural elements and decorative details in masonry churches (roofing shingles, attached galleries, porches, stairs).

Vologda Cathedral of the Savior, Savior-Prilutsky Monastery. 1537–42. Northeast view.

Novgorod   Churches of the Archangel Michael and Annunciation on the Trading Side.
Mid sixteenth century. East view.

Pskov   Church of the Epiphany across the Pskov. 1496. Southwest view.

CHURCH OF THE EPIPHANY ACROSS THE PSKOV RIVER. PSKOV

Very few of the some forty churches built in Pskov during the fifteenth century are extant, but they provide evidence of new developments, such as the proliferation of chapels and galleries around the main cuboid structure. Perhaps the most striking change—one peculiar to Pskov—was a new roof design, introduced as wood planks became the preferred roofing material. This led to a multi-planar covering divided into segments whose level corresponded to the vaulting (the corner segments, for example, were lower than the central gable). Novgorod, by contrast, evolved a trefoil facade and roofline for a similar structure. Ultimately the complex sixteen-sloped roofs in Pskov proved impractical and they yielded toward the end to the century to simpler forms. Among the remaining fifteenth-century churches, the largest and most complex is the Church of the Epiphany across the Pskov River (1496), now devoid of the east chapels that complemented this symmetrically planned structure. The symmetry is, however, broken at the west facade by a great belfry, whose open gables and massive pillars make it one of the most impressive examples of this distinctive Pskovian form.

CHURCH OF ST. NICHOLAS ON THE DRY SPOT. PSKOV

A more typical integration of belfry and church in Pskov is exemplified by the Church of St. Nicholas on the Dry Spot, originally constructed in 1371 and rebuilt in 1535–37. At the time of its completion is was the city's second largest church (after the Trinity Cathedral in the Pskov Kremlin)—a fact now obscured by the accretion of soil to a height of almost two meters above the original ground level.

Pskov   Church of St. Nicholas on the Dry Spot. 1535–57. Northeast view.

A partial restoration of the structure has returned the belfry to its original position above the north facade, where it is particularly effective in mediating the transition from the miniature northeast chapel to the great wood-shingled onion dome above the central structure.

BELL TOWER OF IVAN THE GREAT. MOSCOW KREMLIN

The final, and culminating, monument in the rebuilding of the Kremlin is the Bell Tower of Ivan the Great, begun, like the Archangel Cathedral, in 1505 and completed in 1508. Virtually nothing is known of its architect, Bon Friazin, who had no other recorded structure in Moscow. Yet he was clearly a brilliant engineer, for not only did his bell tower—of 60 meters in two tiers—withstand the fires and other disasters that periodically devastated much of the Kremlin, but it also survived intact a French explosive charge in 1812 strong enough to level two large adjacent structures. The tower, whose height was increased by an additional 21 meters during the reign of Boris Godunov, rests on solid brick walls that are five meters thick at the base and 2.5 meters on the second tier. In addition the walls of the first tier are reinforced by iron beams set within the masonry. Bon Friazin also understood the virtues of simplicity. The facades of the octagonal structure are recessed in the center, with an arcade strip at the top of the panels and a modest ornamental brick cornice, with dentilation, above each tier.

CHURCH OF THE ASCENSION AT KOLOMENSKOE. MOSCOW

The first of Muscovy's great tower churches, the Ascension at Kolomenskoe, was commissioned by Basil III in 1529 as a votive offering for the birth of an heir, Ivan IV. Not only is it of unprecedented height—both in absolute terms and in relation to the size of the floor plan—it also culminates in an elongated brick conical roof (the *shatior*, or "tent" roof) rather than the cupolar form traditionally required in Russian churches). The impression of the Church of the Ascension was intensified by its site on a steep bank above the Moscow River with a dramatic view of the princely domains. Its location in the middle of a compound of wooden structures, including a large palace of haphazard form (burned in 1571 and twice rebuilt), created an ensemble whose silhouette was undoubtedly richer than it is today, when the surviving masonry monuments stand in isolation.

The distinctive form of the Church of the Ascension, and in particular its "tent" roof over an octagonal tower on an attenuated cruciform base, has led to frequent comparisons with the design of Russian wooden tower churches. Other historians argue that the tent form represented a late development of Romanesque (or Gothic) towers with pyramidal roofs. Yet the imaginative leap implied in so bold a design at Kolomenskoe eludes a final explanation. What is ultimately significant is the ingenuity—both Italian and Russian—that allowed the form to appear in brick. Although the technical problems of balancing so much vertical weight had been successfully addressed by Bon Friazin in the Bell Tower of Ivan the Great, the plan of the Ascension Church is more complex, with its cruciform plan and unusual roof.

Moscow   Bell tower of Ivan the Great, Kremlin. 1505–08. Southwest view.

Moscow   Church of the Ascension at Kolomenskoe. 1529–32. Southeast view.

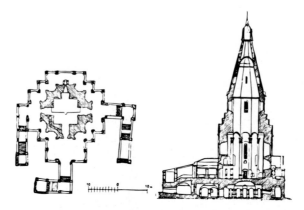

Moscow   Church of the Ascension at Kolomenskoe. Section, plan.

Thus it has been argued that another Italian master—most likely Petrok Malyi—designed this technically demanding structure. The walls, which rest on massive brick cross vaults reinforced with iron tie rods, vary in thickness between 2.5 and 3 meters, and they are further supported by the buttressing effect of the cruciform configuration. The raised terrace (originally without a roof) girding the lower part of the church is reached by three staircases, each with a perpendicular turn that would have increased the visual drama of ritual processions. The main block of the tower, edged with massive pilasters, leads upward to three tiers of pointed *kokoshniki* whose design is echoed in the cornice of the octagon. From this point the

Moscow   Church of the Ascension at Kolomenskoe. West facade, detail.

Moscow   Church of the Ascension at Kolomenskoe. Interior.

"tent" ascends in a pyramidal shape of eight facets delineated by limestone ribs. The rise is accentuated by a rhomboid pattern, also in limestone, that narrows toward the culmination of each facet. The tower concludes with an octagonal lantern, a cupola, and, at the height of 58 meters, a cross.

Italian elements can also be seen on the exterior facades of the Church of the Ascension. Although it has no entablature, the Ascension church has an abundance of elements that point to a knowledge of decorative forms from the Renaissance and, interestingly, from the Gothic. Many of the decorative details also appear on the church interior, which emphasizes the vertical to even more dramatic effect. The basic plan is a square with a side dimension of 8.5 meters—a limited space that does not permit free-standing piers. The piers are, however, recast as pilasters attached at the intersections of the shallow arms of the cross and the main structure, thus dividing each wall into three segments with a framed recessed bay in the center. The capitals of these shafts serve as a spring point for arches that effect the transition from the square to the octagon and, ultimately, to the tent roof.

CHURCH OF THE DECAPITATION OF JOHN THE BAPTIST, AT DIAKOVO. MOSCOW

Within two decades of the completion of the Church of the Ascension, Vasily III's heir, Ivan IV (1529–1584), had commissioned another votive church related to the fortunes of the dynasty. The date of construction is unclear, but it presumably

Moscow   Church of the Decapitation of John the Baptist at Diakovo. Mid 16th century. Southwest view.

occurred between Ivan's coronation, in 1547, and the birth of his son Ivan in 1554. Situated at Diakovo, a village attached to the grand prince's estate of Kolomenskoe and separated from it by a wide ravine, the Church of the Decapitation of John the Baptist rivals the Church of the Ascension in its strikingly innovative form . As with the church at Kolomenskoe, the visual effect of the Diakovo church is enhanced by its location on a bluff overlooking the Moscow River. Although it lacks the vertical *point* provided by the "tent" at Kolomenskoe, the Church of John the Baptist can be classified as another variant of the tower church—the "pillar," or *stolp*—with a massively articulated drum beneath the central dome.

The central structure of the Diakovo church is an octagonal column, each of whose bays is defined not by pilasters—as at Kolomenskoe—but by large doubly recessed panels, reminiscent of the side facades of the Archangel Michael Cathedral by Aleviz. Above the cornice a tier of semicircular *kokoshniki* is surmounted by pediments in a transition to the great drum, whose plastic form is composed of a series of semicylinders placed on a high octagonal base. Despite the unusual appearance of these forms, they function to reduce the weight of the drum without decreasing its strength. The relation of rounded and octagonal volumes, of circular and pointed surfaces, is reinforced by the four ancillary chapels, also octagonal and with a design similar to that of the main tower.

This symmetrical arrangement of small churches around the central mass—all resting on the same base is the most intriguing feature of the Church of John the Baptist. Following the example of his father, Vasily III, Ivan and his clerics dedicated the separate altars as an affirmation of the personal relation between the tsar—as he was now formally called—and the deity. For example, the central church, from which the entire structure derives its name, commemorates a solemn event from the Gospels—an event whose day in the church calendar also served as the nameday of Ivan. Identifying the meaning of the dedications of these ancillary chapels does not, however, account for the form of the Diakovo church. Most large, and many not so large, Russian churches had attached chapels with their own dedications. At Diakovo the subsidiary chapels were part of a highly inte-

Moscow   Church of the Decapitation of John the Baptist at Diakovo. Section, plan.

Moscow   Church of the Decapitation of John the Baptist at Diakovo. Interior.

grated design that reproduced the central form at the four corners of a square base, and the linked the five components with a surrounding gallery. The complexity was increased by the presence of a large semicircular apse attached to the main tower but also linked to the two flanking east chapels. The interiors of the towers are each articulated with a clarity that integrates tectonic detail and aesthetic form—as in the corbelled levels of brick effecting the transition from the lower to upper structure.

Although no documentary evidence has been discovered, the architect for this complex structure probably came from Pskov—not only because of the long tradition of Pskov collectives at work in the Moscow area and their highly-regarded skill as brick masons, but also from certain features suggestive of the Pskov style, such as the open belfry on the west facade. Furthermore, there is evidence concerning masons from Pskov in service to Ivan IV as fortification engineers and as architects within Moscow itself, most notably of the Cathedral of the Intercession on the Moat (St. Basil's).

PIATNITSKY GATE OF THE KOLOMNA KREMLIN

During his reign grand prince Vasily III initiated a number of major fortification projects, among which one of the most impressive was the fortress (kremlin) of the town of Kolomna, 115 kilometers to the southeast of Moscow. By the eighteenth century, the brick walls had become decrepit; and over the next century, most sections were dismantled for building material. Early groups of preservationists were able, however, to save a few of the most important structures. The Piatnitsky Gate, on the east side, originally formed the main entrance into the fortress, and the only

Kolomna   Piatnitsky Gate, Kolomna Kremlin.

rival to this structure in size and complexity of design is the Borovitsky Gate of the Moscow kremlin.

CHURCH OF THE DORMITION, BRUSENSKY MONASTERY. KOLOMNA

The most remarkable structure of Brusensky Monastery (largely rebuilt in the nineteenth century) is the Dormition Church, commissioned by Ivan the Terrible to commemorate his greatest victory, the taking of Kazan in 1552. Built in the same year, this church demonstrates Ivan's fondness for the tent tower form, which would be applied shortly thereafter on a much larger and more complex scale in the church popularly known as St. Basil's—also commemorating the victory over Kazan. The small Dormition Church is, perhaps, a direct precursor of the great Moscow shrine.

CATHEDRAL OF THE INTERCESSION ON THE MOAT (ST. BASIL'S).

The fame of the building that has come to epitomize the extravagance of Muscovite imagination rests on more than its colorful exterior. The notorious character of Ivan IV (the Terrible)—who commissioned the Cathedral of the Intercession in 1555 as a commemoration of his taking of Kazan in 1552—and the savagery of the latter part of his reign have fostered the notion of a structure devoid of restraint or reason. Yet the architects of record, Barma and Postnik Yakovlev (the latter from Pskov), created a thoroughly coherent, logical plan. The

Kolomna   Church of the Dormition, Brusensky Monastery. 1552. East view.

Cathedral of the Intercession consists of a central tower flanked by ancillary free-standing churches in an alternating pattern of major and minor forms: minor on the diagonal and major at the compass points.

The octagonal motif at the base of the plan is repeated in the drum and tent roof of the central tower, as well as in the four octagonal churches on the compass points. The four smaller churches are cuboid (a shape obscured by the seventeenth-century enclosure of the terrace surrounding the cathedral), and are surmounted by a cupola and round drum raised on three tiers of *kokoshniki*. The height of their onion domes is carefully measured to compliment those of the larger churches. Within this interrelation of forms, the silhouette of the cathedral conveys considerably different impressions of its shape, depending on the

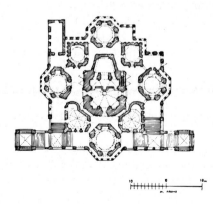

Moscow   Cathedral of the Intercession on the Moat. Plan.

Moscow   Cathedral of the Intercession on the Moat, Red Square. 1555–61. South view.

Moscow   Cathedral of the Intercession on the Moat. West view.

Moscow   Cathedral of the Intercession on the Moat. East view.

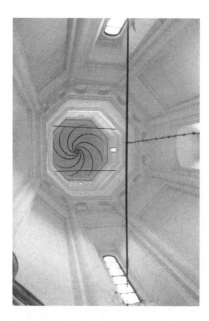

Moscow   Cathedral of the Intercession on the Moat. Interior.

approach and perspective of the viewer. The west side, containing flanking stairways that ascend to the entrance to the ensemble, has, appropriately, the quality of
a frontal facade, as though of a monolithic structure.

In contrast a viewing of the cathedral from the river (to the south) or from Red
Square (the north) presents a multi-axial shape, not only because of the accrual
of other structures such as the bell tower on the southeast corner, but in the very
nature of the design, which like much great architecture, includes a calculated
distortion: the central tower is not in the geometric center of the plan, but is
shifted substantially westward to accommodate the apsidal structure. Indeed,
the main church tower is the only one of the nine to have such a substantial addition. To accommodate this shift the small chapels on the west lose the interior
corner of their cube and are reduced to a size only large enough to contain a
handful of worshippers. Thus, seen from the north or south the Cathedral of the
Intercession has a dual center: that of the tower itself and that of the structure as
a whole.

CATHEDRAL OF ST. SOPHIA (DIVINE WISDOM). VOLOGDA

The symbolic uses of the Kremlin Dormition Cathedral are again revealed in the
building of the main cathedral of Vologda, a major trading and administrative
center in the north of Russia during the sixteenth and seventeenth centuries. Ivan
IV devoted much attention to Vologda in the late 1560s, during the period of the
oprichnina, when the tsar created his personal state within Muscovy. An essential
part of the enhancement of Vologda was the building of a major cathedral for the
bishopric that was transferred to the city in 1571. Although modeled on

Vologda   Cathedral of St. Sophia. 1568–70. Southeast view.

Fioravanti's Dormition Cathedral, the Vologda cathedral was dedicated the Divine Sophia—a reflection of Vologda's rivalry with Novgorod, whose religious as well as secular power had been steadily reduced by Moscow's rulers.

   Having appropriated the name of Novgorod's great cathedral, the architects of the Vologda cathedral effected a remarkably graceful, simplified interpretation of the Moscow Dormition, with pilaster strips leading to a horizontal row of four zakomary, above which are five domes. Of the major Dormition offspring, the Vologda cathedral bears the closest resemblance to the cathedral at the Novodevichy Convent. The interior of St. Sophia—with a particularly vivid "Last Judgement" on the west wall—was painted in 1686–1688 by a group of some thirty artists from Yaroslavl led by the same Dmitry Grigorev (or Plekhanov) who supervised the painting of the Dormition Cathedral at the Trinity-Sergius Monastery.

CATHEDRAL OF THE SMOLENSK MOTHER OF GOD, NOVODEVICHY CONVENT. MOSCOW

Founded by Basil III to commemorate the annexation of the city of Smolensk within the Russian state in 1514, the Novodevichy Convent has as its central element a cathedral dedicated to the Icon of the Smolensk Mother of God. Of the

Moscow   Cathedral of the Smolensk Mother of God, Novodevichy Convent. 1524–25; rebuilt latter half of 16th century(?). South view.

early sixteenth-century Muscovite cathedrals, this church impresses with the height of its four longitudinal bays. In contrast to the Kremlin Dormition Cathedral and a number of its successors, the main zakomara of each facade of the Smolensk Cathedral is distinguished by greater height as well as width—thus signifying the arms of the inscribed cross. The verticality is further developed by elevating the church above a ground floor which served as a burial chamber for wealthy nobles or members of the princely family. The vertical emphasis of the Smolensk Cathedral culminates in massed onion domes, whose peaks support gilded crosses of a height commensurate with the proportions of the drums and cupolas. In view of the similarity of this form to other large churches of the 1560s and 1570s, it is now argued that the cathedral was expanded to its present form during that period.

CATHEDRAL OF THE NATIVITY OF THE VIRGIN, LUZHETSKY MONASTERY. MOZHAISK

Founded in 1408 by Saint Ferapont in a minor principality to the west of Moscow, the Luzhetsky Monastery was frequently rebuilt after a number of fires and invasions. Nonetheless, the Cathedral of the Nativity (1540s)—the

Mozhaisk   Cathedral of the Nativity of the Virgin, Luzhetsky Monastery. Mid 16th century. Southeast view.

monastery's main, and oldest, building—has survived relatively intact and exemplifies the purity of form in monastic church architecture during the early reign of Ivan the Terrible. Elevated on a high base, the brick, cuboid structure has three bays on each facade and culminates in five cupolas with wooden shingles. The detailing accents structural elements without assuming an overtly ornamental character.

CHURCH OF THE DORMITION, SAVIOR-EVFIMY MONASTERY. SUZDAL

The largest of Suzdal's monasteries is the Savior-Evfimy, whose refectory Church of the Dormition, formerly dated to 1525, now appears to have been constructed no earlier than the last quarter of the century. The uniquely Russian institution of refectory churches flourished in the 17th century and seems to have begun as austere structures with no differentiated altar space attached, exemplified by the refectory Church of the Conception of St. Anne (1551) at the Intercession Convent in Suzdal. The Savior-Evfimy refectory, however, has a clearly defined church structure with a distinctive tent tower above rows of *kokoshniki*, as well as an apse and attached chapel on the southeast. Its roofing of wooden shingles is the result of a recent restoration.

CHURCH OF THE CRUCIFIXION, ALEKSANDROVA SLOBODA

Early in his reign Basil III established a new compound on a favored site for hunting and pilgrimage to the north of Moscow. Called Aleksandrova Sloboda, the

Suzdal   Refectory Church of the Dormition, Savior-Evfimy Monastery. Late 16th century. Southeast view.

Aleksandrov   Bell tower and Church of the Crucifixion, Aleksandrova Sloboda. 1570s. Southeast view.

walled compound with its lodges and ancillary buildings centered around the Cathedral of the Intercession, built in 1513 to a design resembling that of the Intercession Cathedral in Suzdal. In 1565 Ivan IV designated the site the center of his state within a state, and held grotesque court here. In the mid-1570s, an early sixteenth-century octagonal bell tower was encased within the massive pylons of a two-story polygonal arcade, supporting three tiers of *kokoshniki*, an open octagon, and a tent roof with cupola soaring to a height of 56 meters. With this monument Ivan not only provided Aleksandrova Sloboda with the vertical dominant characteristic of Russian monastic ensembles but also commemorated his own apocalyptic rule from this compound. The innovation of the structure (dedicated at the end of the seventeenth century to the Crucifixion) lay in the adaptation of the "tent" form to the bell tower—a device that would spread throughout Russian church architecture in the following century.

CHURCH OF THE TRANSFIGURATION AT OSTROV. MOSCOW REGION

The vitality of the tent tower form in late sixteenth-century architecture is nowhere more forcefully stated than in the Church of the Transfiguration at the village of Ostrov, another country estate of the grand princes, and later tsars, on the southern outskirts of Moscow. In the absence of documentation, much in the construc-

Moscow region   Church of the Transfiguration at Ostrov. Late 16th c. South view.

tion history of this church remains unclear, including its date of completion. The central part of the lower church is a massive limestone cruciform structure, reminiscent of the Ascension at Kolomenskoe yet substantially different in the configuration of its east, apsidal end. Whereas the Kolomenskoe church had no apse, the church at Ostrov reveals a pronounced extension of the eastern end, which produces on the interior a less coherent delineation of space than at Kolomenskoe.

Much of the exterior ornament at Ostrov, and particularly the arcade frieze beneath the cornice of the central structure, represents a revival of romanesque motifs, while the decorative detail of the upper part of the apses is derived from the architecture of Pskov. The massed banks of *kokoshniki* on both the corner chapels and, in two tiers, on the central tower illustrates the transformation of a form that had once served clearly to delineate the verticality of structure, as at Kolomenskoe, but would acquire a diminished, decorative function in the late sixteenth and early seventeenth centuries.

CATHEDRAL OF THE DON MOTHER OF GOD, DONSKOI MONASTERY. MOSCOW

The influence and wealth of Boris Godunov were reflected in a building program that began during the late 1580s and resulted in a "Godunov style" of

Moscow   Cathedral of the Don Mother of God, Donskoi Monastery. 1593. Southeast view.

church—a single-cupola structure, often with no interior piers, and a pyramidal bank of *kokoshniki* above the main cornice. A developed example of the style appeared no later than 1593 with the completion at Donskoi Monastery of the Small Cathedral of the Don Mother of God (so named to distinguish it from the monastery's large cathedral with the same dedication built at the end of the seventeenth century). Located at the southern approaches to Moscow, Donskoi Monastery was the last of the major monastic strongpoints constructed to defend the medieval city. In 1591 an army of the Crimean khan Kazy-Girei made a full-scale raid on Moscow; and at a site between the Kaluga and Tula roads leading to the south of the city, Boris Godunov deployed a movable wooden fortress to protect his forward artillery. Godunov subsequently achieved a spectacular victory over the invading forces—the last Tatar raid ever to reach the outskirts of Moscow. After the rout Godunov donated much of the considerable wealth conferred upon him for his military leadership to the foundation of a monastery on the location of his mobile fort.

The Donskoi monastery cathedral, while not on the scale and in the dramatic form of votive churches built during the reigns of Basil III and Ivan the Terrible, nonetheless follows a pattern of celebratory architecture, dynamic in its emphasis on the upward movement of form in a pyramid of *kokoshniki* etched in white on a background of painted stucco over brick. The vertical development of the cathedral has long been obscured by two attached chapels flanking the apse, a refectory,

 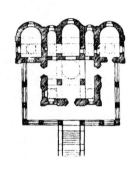

Viaziomy   Church of the Trinity. Section, plan.

and bell tower—all added in the 1670s. From the east side, however, the unobstructed central form provides a sense of the proportional relation between the original structure and the three tiers beneath the drum, which is supported on the interior by corbelled arches within a domical vault.

CHURCH OF THE TRINITY AT VIAZIOMY. MOSCOW REGION

Many of the same motifs reappear on a larger scale at the Church of the Trinity built in the late 1590s on the estate of Boris Godunov at Viaziomy. Elevated on a high limestone base, the this building (renamed the Transfiguration of the Savior at the end of the seventeenth century) retains the semicircular niches of the smaller churches, but places them within a more traditional and monumental pentacupolar design whose facade is articulated in the manner of Aleviz. In addition to the precise delineation of the facade bays by pilasters and the double segmentation of the cornice, the Viaziomy architect paid homage to the Italian master in the brilliant use of profiled arches at the upper level of each bay, thus emphasizing the verticality of the structure.

Indeed, the Viaziomy church uses the visual language not only of the Archangel Michael Cathedral, but also of Fioravanti's Dormition Cathedral. As in the latter, the walls are of limestone up to the cornice level, with brick for the vaulting and cupola drums; and the original roof, covered with oak shingles, followed the contours of the semicircular *zakomary*. On the east side, the central structure is flanked by two chapels that are skilfully integrated into the main structure by a raised terrace, and by a pyramid of *kokoshniki* leading to a small cupola over each chapel.

Moscow region Church of the Trinity at Viaziomy. 1598(?). West view.

7. THE SEVENTEENTH CENTURY

CHURCH OF THE TRINITY IN NIKITNIKI. MOSCOW

After the interregnum known as the Time of Troubles, at the beginning of the 17th century, the national recovery seemed to call forth elaborate exterior decoration, exemplified by the Church of the Trinity in Nikitniki, situated on a lane in Moscow's Kitai-gorod. Endowed by the merchant Grigory Nikitnikov, the church consists of a central cube with five cupolas and no interior piers—an indication both of its modest size and of the flexible possibilities of brick construction. After its completion in 1634, the original pentacupolar structure acquired over the next two decades two chapels (attached at the northeast and southeast) and an enclosed gallery leading to a bell tower with tent roof on the northwest corner. This is the earliest example of the placement of a bell tower within the church ensemble—a practice that would become generally accepted in parish architecture in the seventeenth century. At the corner of the bell tower the gallery turns at a right angle and descends by a covered staircase to a porch at the southwest corner, capped by *kokoshniki* and yet another pyramidal roof. The south Chapel of Nikita (St. Nicetas) the Warrior served as the family burial chapel.

CHURCH OF THE DORMITION, MONASTERY OF ST. ALEKSY. UGLICH

The increasing complexity of seventeenth-century tower churches is evident in the refectory Church of the Dormition (1628) at the Monastery of St. Aleksy in Uglich. Known in contemporary accounts as *Divnaia* (the wondrous) Church for the daring structure and harmony of its three tent spires, the unusual design is derived from the builder's placement of the towers not only over the central cube but also above the two flanking chapels on the east end, suggesting a possible symbolic reference to the Trinity. Although there is no specific votive dedication, the fact that the church arose as part of a rebuilding of the monastery after its opposition to and sack by the Poles during the Time of Troubles is sufficient to characterize its form as an architectural memorial to national deliverance, particularly since the towers admit almost no light to the cramped interior. Attached to the church on the west

Moscow　Church of the Trinity in Nikitniki. 1628–51. Southwest view.

Uglich   Church of the Dormition, Monastery of St. Aleksy. 1628. East view.

is a large refectory that provides a counterweight with its simple and massive rectangular form.

CHURCH OF SAINTS ZOSIMA AND SAVVATY, TRINITY-ST. SERGIUS MONASTERY. SERGIEV POSAD

One of the most imposing of the early seventeenth-century tower churches is the Church of Sts. Zosima and Savvaty (1635–1637) at the Trinity-St. Sergius Monastery. By virtue of its great role in the national revival during the Time of Troubles, the monastery received lavish gifts to supported its expansion and the repair of the damage inflicted during the monastery's resistance to a Polish siege between September 1608 and January 1610. As part of that rebuilding, the Church of Sts. Zosima and Savvaty honors two monks who in the first half of the fifteenth century were among the founders of the Monastery of the Transfiguration on the Solovetsk Islands in the White Sea. Because both monasteries repulsed foreign invaders during the Time of Troubles, the dedication of this church to the founders of the Solovetsk monastery implies both a monastic and a military alliance.

In addition the location of the Church of Sts. Zosima and Savvaty, rising from a space created on the second story of the monastery infirmary, signifies the charitable role of the monks in accepting and treating great numbers of

Sergiev Posad   Church of Saints Zosima and Savvaty, Trinity-St. Sergius Monastery.
1635–37. Southeast view.

wounded from Moscow after the Polish suppression of an uprising in the city in
the March 1611. The tent tower of the church, rising over the northwest wall (in
the direction of Solovetsk), served as a memorial not only to the wounded and
dying from all of the campaigns but also to those who distinguished themselves
during the siege of the monastery itself—represented in depictions of cannons
and soldiers on a number of the green ceramic tiles that decorate the tent. The
tent tower is isolated from the rest of the structure by a vaulted ceiling (at the
base of the *zakomary*), which permitted the heating of the church for use in all
seasons of the year.

CHURCH OF THE HODIGITRIA ICON, MONASTERY OF JOHN THE BAPTIST. VIAZMA

Founded in 1536 on a hill above the Beber River, the Monastery of John the
Baptist has undergone the many trials of this frequently invaded land: it was
burned by Polish detachments during the Time of Troubles in the early seventeenth century; rebuilt in the 1630s with a donation from Tsar Mikhail Fedorovich
(the first Romanov tsar); burned again during the Napoleonic invasion of 1812;
repaired in 1832–36; closed after the bolshevik revolution; and further damaged
during the Second World War. Nonetheless, its seventeenth-century churches
were so well built as to remain structurally sound, including one of the most
striking monuments of late medieval Russia: the Church of the Hodigitria Icon

Viazma   Church of the Hodigitria Icon, Monastery of John the Baptist. 1635–38.
Southeast view.

(1635–38), with its massive brick base, ascending tiers of *kokoshniki*, and three towers. On either side of the apse are two additional chapels with cupolas. To the west is a one-story vestibule, necessary for the functioning of the church but modest in comparison with the main structure. Perhaps this exuberant design represent a beacon, as its dedication suggests. Or Perhaps it commemorates resistance to invaders, as do other tower churches built in Muscovy following the Time of Troubles. Due to the destruction of the interior in 1812, nothing remains of the original frescoes.

CHURCH OF ELIJAH THE PROPHET. YAROSLAVL

The most renowned of Yaroslavl's seventeenth-century monuments is the Church of Elijah the Prophet, located on the central square of the city. The donors of the Elijah church, the Skripin brothers, possessed great wealth gained from the Siberian fur trade, and they had access both to the tsar and to the patriarch. In 1647 they endowed the building of a pentacupolar brick church on an elevated base that also supported an enclosed gallery. The roofline of the main structure originally followed the contours of the arched gables, which are still visible despite a simplification of the roof design typical in the 18th century. Like many churches of its period the Elijah Church had chapels flanking the apse on the east, of which the north chapel represents a small self-contained church with a pyramid of *kokoshniki* beneath its cupola. The balanced asymmetry of the ensemble is most clearly stated, however, in the two towers attached to the west of the structure: the bell tower at the northwest corner; and the sep-

Yaroslavl   Church of the Prophet Elijah. 1647–50. West view.

arate Chapel of the Deposition of the Robe, at the southwest corner, culminating in a tent tower roof.

Thirty years after the completion of the church in 1650, the widow of one of the Skripin brothers commissioned the painting of the interior of the main church by two of the most accomplished fresco artists in seventeenth-century Russia—Gury Nikitin and Sila Savin. These splendid frescoes are among the best-preserved in Russia and are particularly valuable as an illustration of the growing secular influence in Russian religious art during the late seventeenth-century. The exterior of the structure was painted with elaborate decorative motifs similar to those added in the same period to Moscow's Cathedral of the Intercession on the Moat.

OLD ENGLISH COURT. MOSCOW

In Moscow the best surviving example of masonry architecture for mercantile purposes is the Old English Court, first built in the early sixteenth century for the merchant Ivan Bobrishchev (the lower walls, of limestone, remain). Ivan the Terrible subsequently made the building available to English merchants after the negotiation of an Anglo-Russian trade agreement in 1556. The building was frequently modified; and after the expulsion of the English merchants in 1649, it passed through a succession of owners. The Old English Court has now been restored to its appearance at the first half of the seventeenth century, when it contained offices and storage rooms for the company. Its form is largely functional, and yet the use of decorative recessed panels, or *shirinki*, and the central bay and steps exemplify the decorative asymmetry of the medieval Russian buildings. There were in fact several such brick structures built in Kitai-Gorod during the seventeenth century, particularly after the issuance of an edict in 1681 forbidding wooden construction in the central parts of the city. Nonethe-less, Moscow's buildings, with the exception of churches, remained primarily of logs.

CHURCH OF THE TWELVE APOSTLES, KREMLIN. MOSCOW

Commissioned by Patriarch Nikon as part of the Patriarchal Palace in the Moscow Kremlin, this large church was originally dedicated to the Apostle Phillip, in implicit homage to the Metropolitan Phillip, who had achieved mar-

Moscow   Old English Court. Early 16th and 17th centuries. South view.

Moscow   Church of the Twelve Apostles, Kremlin. 1652–56. South view.

tyrdom for his opposition to the terror of Ivan IV. The design and detailing of this large brick church, built in 1652–1656, were derived from the twelfth-century limestone churches of Vladimir. Nikon intended that his church serve as a model for the return to the symbolically correct forms of church design. Of particular significance was the pentacupolar design with low domes. Noticeably absent were all references to the onion dome and to the tent tower, which had gained such popularity in Russian votive and parish churches. By 1655 Nikon and his hierarchs had condemned the tent form as inappropriate for the Orthodox church, although it was permitted for bell towers. His reasons for so doing lay not only in a desire to return the church to the purity of its pre-Mongol forms, but also to curtail the diversity of essentially secular, commemorative interpretations of the tower.

CATHEDRAL OF THE RESURRECTION. NEW JERUSALEM

In 1657 Patriarch Nikon proposed the idea of building a re-creation of the Anastasia, or Church of the Resurrection in Jerusalem, at a picturesque site on the Istra River, to the west of Moscow. The cathedral was to be the center of the Monastery of the Resurrection at New Jerusalem, with a tiered gate church dedicated to the Entry of Christ into Jerusalem. Nikon received support in this visionary plan from Tsar Aleksei, and by 1658 construction was well underway. To guide his builders Nikon had available various sources of information on the Jerusalem shrine, of which the most important seems to have been the published

Istra Monastery of the Resurrection, New Jerusalem. Gate Church of the Entry into Jerusalem. 1690–94. Southwest view.

description, with illustrations and plans, of the holy monuments in Jerusalem by Bernadino Amico. As in its Jerusalem prototype, the Resurrection Cathedral contained several components, including the church proper, a bell tower, and attached chapels with cupolas, all situated to the east of the rotunda.

Although work was halted at New Jerusalem after Nikon was sent into exile by a church council in 1666, the project was resumed in 1679 at the command of Tsar Fedor. After the completion of the cathedral in 1684, surrounding wooden structures in the monastery were rebuilt of brick in the ornamental "Moscow Baroque" style. The cathedral itself had a significant influence in the development of some of the most distinctive features of that style, including the revival of centralized tower churches and certain forms of exterior ornamentation of western provenance. Despite its impressive engineering, the rotunda and brick roof collapsed in 1723 as the result of a failure of the westernmost wall. In 1756–1761 the rotunda walls were repaired and the conical roof rebuilt in wood by Karl Blank, with projecting baroque window surrounds. During the same period Bartolomeo Francesco Rastrelli redid the interior in a florid late baroque style, which stood until the end of 1941, when the cathedral was severely damaged by the German army during the battle of Moscow.

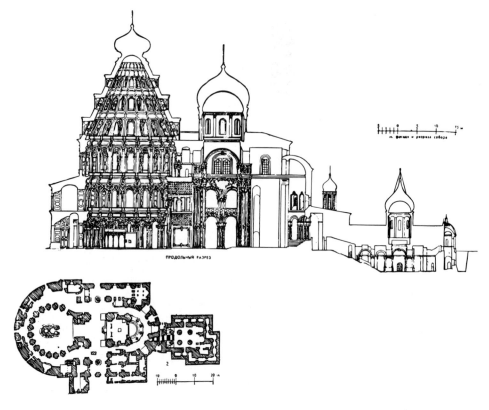

Istra   Cathedral of the Resurrection at New Jerusalem. Section, plan.

ST. KIRILL-BELOZERSK MONASTERY. KIRILLOV

Founded in 1397 by Kirill, a monk from Moscow, this monastery, located near White Lake (Beloe ozero), occupied a strategically important position for Moscow's expansion into the far north. It therefore received major donations that by the sixteenth century made it one of the largest of Russian monasteries, second in size to the Trinity-St. Sergius Monastery near Moscow. Indeed, both monasteries played a significant role in defending Russian territory during the Time of Troubles. The first of its extant brick structures, the Dormition Cathedral (1496), has been much altered, as have most of the monastery's other churches and chapels, built during the sixteenth and eighteenth centuries. The most imposing feature of the monastery complex (actually composed of two adjacent monasteries—the Dormition and John the Baptist—as well as a settlement for lay workers) is its system of walls, rebuilt between 1653 and the 1680s with the help of a generous grant from Tsar Aleksei Mikhailovich. Ironically, the monastery never faced another military threat, and its walls and towers now stand as further testimony to the Russian ability to erect masonry structures of enormous extent during the late medieval period.

Istra Cathedral, Monastery of the Resurrection, New Jerusalem. 1658–85; rebuilt mid-18th century.

CHURCH OF ST. NICHOLAS IN KHAMOVNIKI. MOSCOW

As an increasing number of parishes replaced wooden with brick churches in the seventeenth century, there arose a type of design known as the "ship," with a bell tower (the prow) in the west, connected by a low refectory to the main structure, with five cupolas and an apse in the east. The durability of the "ship" form of church persisted into the eighteenth century, despite the dramatic changes in church design over the same period. Not only did it provide an easily assimilated model that could be reproduced by builders in the country as well as in a confined urban setting, but it also allowed for inexhaustible variations in detail. One of the best examples of the form is the Church of St. Nicholas in Khamovniki (1679–1682), built for the wealthy settlement of weavers located in this southwest district of Moscow. The prosperity of the guild is evident in the decoration of the church, whose main structure retains the complex layering of *kokoshniki*. The attached columns and consoles supporting the *zakomary*, as well as the decorative window surrounds, are all outlined in bright polychrome on a background of whitewashed brick. The same use of color extends to the magnificent bell tower—one of the tallest attached to a church in Moscow—whose height allowed both a greater distribution of sound and a surface for the display of decorative devices such as ornamental dormer windows on the tent tower.

Istra   Cathedral of the Resurrection. Interior.

Kirillov   St. Kirill-Belozersk Monastery St. Ferapont Tower and walls of the New Fort. 1654–80.

Moscow Church of St. Nicholas in Khamovniki. 1679–82. South view.

CHURCH OF THE TRINITY AT OSTANKINO. MOSCOW

One of the most elaborate examples of ornamental church design in the late seventeenth century is the Church of the Trinity on the Cherkassky family estate of Ostankino to the north of Moscow (1678–1683). The Ostankino church is notable both for its size (unusually large for an estate church) and for its idiosyncratic decorative motifs. Instead of whitewash and polychrome, the builder (identified as the serf master Pavel Potekhin) exploited the decorative contrast of molded brick and limestone detail, which is particularly striking in the window surrounds and the structural detail on the east facade. The bell tower was added in 1832, but did not receive its conical "tent" until a restoration of the church in 1878. There are no interior piers. Parts of the iconostasis date to the late seventeenth century.

CHURCH OF THE TRINITY. SERPUKHOV

Serpukhov, 102 kilometers south of Moscow, still offers vistas that suggest the medieval when the town was one of Muscovy's major southern defensive posts on the Oka River. Almost all of Serpukhov's surviving sixteenth-century walls were dismantled in 1933 for use as building material in the first line of the Moscow subway. A few churches in the town center have been well repaired and are in active use. The early eighteenth-century Church of Trinity, for example, offers an excellent example of the durability of the "ship" form, with a slender bell tower in the

Moscow   Church of the Trinity in Ostankino. 1678–83. East view.

west. Its vestibule was rebuilt in the nineteenth century, and additional rows of decorative *kokoshniki* were hidden in a modification of the roof. Although provincial and anonymous in design, this structure illustrates the harmony and balance achieved even in typical parish churches at the end of the "medieval" period in Russian architecture.

CHURCH OF JOHN THE BAPTIST AT TOLCHKOVO. YAROSLAVL

Of the many churches built by neighborhood guilds in Yaroslavl during the late seventeenth century, perhaps the most elaborate is the Church of John the Baptist at Tolchkovo, constructed between 1671 and 1687 with funds provided largely by Rodion and Leonty Yeremin, whose wealth derived from leather workshops located in the district. Its plan included an enclosed gallery on three sides of the rectangular structure and two symmetrical chapels at each eastern corner. Entrance porches with steeply-pitched roofs mark the center of the north, west, and south galleries. The spacing of clusters of attached columns as a decorative means of segmenting the facades had been introduced at the Resurrection Cathedral (1670–1678) of the neighboring town of Tutaev, but at Tolchkovo their symmetrical placement occurs within a melange of decorative elements, such as miniature pointed arches over paired columns of molded patterned brick, and represents the triumph of saturated ornament over the clarity of individual ele-

Serpukhov   Church of the Trinity. Early 18th century. Northwest view.

ments. The elaborate forms of the brick were complemented by bright polychrome tiles on the facade. Indeed, the decorative relief work of the upper tiers can only with difficulty be distinguished from the colorful trompe l'oeil rustication on the apsidal structure. Greater ingenuity is shown in the design of the east chapels, whose cornice is elevated to the height of the main structure. This creates not only a uniform roof level, but also gives the east facade a monumental unity, with two additional accent points in each chapel's miniature groupings of five cupolas on elongated drums.

The interiors of the chapels and the main church contained intricately carved iconostases complemented by frescoes that also extended throughout the attached galleries. Painted under the supervision of the Yaroslavl master Dmitry Grigorev Plekhanov between 1694 and 1700, the frescoes portray biblical motifs in a contemporary secular setting. Although fanciful Western architectural motifs frequently dominate the background of these wall paintings, the figures themselves and the details of the biblical scenes indicate an unambiguous approval of the prosperous commercial milieu of Iaroslavl.

The Church of John the Baptist also had ancillary structures, including a separate winter church (not extant) and an entrance framed by a Holy Gate. The dominant feature of the ensemble is the campanile, built at the turn of the eighteenth century in the florid style known as "Moscow Baroque." 45 meters in height, the

Yaroslavl   Church of John the Baptist at Tolchkovo. 1671–87. East view.

bell tower is decorated with limestone elements, including balusters and pinnacles that emphasize the ascending octagons—an amalgam of Russian and Dutch design.

CHURCH OF THE EPIPHANY. YAROSLAVL

The Church of the Epiphany was built near the west wall of the Savior Monastery in 1684–1693 with funds provided by the merchant Aleksei Zubchaninov. With an emphasis on the vertical, the structure makes rich use of ceramic decoration on a background of brick walls painted dark red. Despite the one-story gallery around the base of the church and the bell tower, the vertical ascent is clearly stated by the elongated window shafts framed in pilasters, which are decorated with a string of polychrome tiles set diagonally. The tops of the window shafts end a slight ogival point that is repeated in the three tiers of arched gables above the cornice. In counterpoint to this vertical emphasis, the horizontal lines of the church are defined with bright ceramic tiles that culminate in the profiled entablature at the top of the walls. The tiles are of two sorts: a repeated ornamental element used for architectural details such as the architrave; and a series of five square tiles, each of which contains a different design. These five variations are multiplied by five different color patterns. The Epiphany Church thus combines the Yaroslavl arrangement of structural components (bell tower, gallery, chapels, and church) with a style of Moscow ornamentalism that began in the late sixteenth century: a pyramid of *kokoshniki* over a cube with no interior piers, and ceramic ornament on the exterior.

Yaroslavl   Church of the Epiphany. 1684–93. Northwest view.

The precise brickwork and the buttressing effect of the exterior gallery at the Epiphany Church permitted larger windows than usual for Russian churches of the late seventeenth century. These provide ample illumination for the interior walls, divided into eight levels of brightly colored frescoes painted in 1692–1693 and devoted primarily to scenes from the life of Christ, with particular emphasis on his teachings and ministry. The lack of interior piers further enhances the perception of the wall paintings, which contain decorative motifs that repeat certain of the ceramic designs of the exterior. The planes of the vault demonstrate the ingenuity of the artists in adapting complex compositions such as the Dormition, the Resurrection, and the Ascension to the curved vaulting surface.

COURT OF THE ROSTOV METROPOLITANATE. ROSTOV KREMLIN

Toward the end of the seventeenth century, Rostov became the site of one of the last, and largest, building projects of medieval Muscovy. Its patron, Metropolitan Jonah, was close to Tsar Aleksei Mikhailovich and marshalled enormous resources for the building of what was in fact an ideal city. Jonah had at his command 16,000 serfs as well as the best craftsmen of his large and prosperous eparchy; and within twenty years—between 1670 and 1690—his masons erected not only several large churches and buildings for the metropolitan's court and residence, but also a magnificent set of walls with towers and gate churches, situated on the north shore of Lake Nero. The adjacent, massive form of the Rostov Dormition Cathedral, provided a monumental scale and design for the metropolitan's compound, to which it is linked visually by the great belfry. Apparently

Rostov   Gate Church of the Resurrection. 1670. Northwest view.

Rostov   Red Chambers. 1672–80

built between 1682 and 1687, the belfry, with interior stairs to the bell gallery, is composed of two adjoining structures, of which the taller (and later) contains the greatest of the bells—the 36-ton "Sysoi," named after Jonah's father. The larger segment of the belfry, with three bays, contains the remaining twelve bells.

From the belfry, the northern entrance to the Kremlin is flanked by two decorative towers with bulbous domes, between which is the north facade of the gate Church of the Resurrection (1670). Its pointed gables, beneath soaring cupolas typical of the Rostov-Yaroslavl area, remind of wooden architectural forms, as does the attached raised gallery along the south facade and west facades of the church. The facades are divided into three bays by pilaster strips, but the builders' imagination is given freer reign in the multitude of arched forms for the various portals on the ground floor and in the gallery arcade above. The interior is without piers (the corner drums of the roof are decorative only), and is entirely covered in frescoes.

Within the walls the main part of the compound is occupied by buildings associated with the metropolitanate, including the Red Chambers or palace (*palata*), used as the metropolitan's residence. Built in the southwest corner of the walls in 1672–1680, the chambers form an L-shaped two-storied structure with a sloped roof typical of large masonry dwellings in the pre-Petrine period. The main, elevated level is reached by a covered porch and steps, with tent towers over the successive landings—another device characteristic to both masonry and wooden domestic architecture in Russia during the seventeenth century, although here implemented on an unusually spacious scale. The interior space contains a large hall supported by a central pillar, as had been used in such ecclesiastical residences since the fifteenth century.

Rostov   Gate Church of St. John the Divine. 1683. West view.

Attached to the palace through a series of passageways was the Church of the Savior on the Stores, built in 1675 above a provisions cellar. The church is simple in its cuboid design with an intersecting gabled roof not unlike wooden architecture of the period; yet because of its proximity to the metropolitan's residence, it served as his personal chapel not only for devotional purposes, but also for the performance of sacred music for the metropolitan and his guests. The interior of the church was decorated with perhaps the richest of wall paintings in the entire compound.

The west wall of the Rostov kremlin contains the ensemble's second major gate church, built in 1683 and dedicated to St. John the Divine. Although similar in design to the Gate Church of the Resurrection, the St. John Church is more elaborately decorated, with a frieze of ogival arches on the upper walls that reproduces the blind arcade on the exterior of the Dormition Cathedral and gives a "gothic" appearance to the structure. The apsidal structure on this, as on all of the kremlin churches built by Jonah, is a low, clearly-defined projection of three bays roofed in wood.

SIUIUMBEKI TOWER. KAZAN

During the latter part of the seventeenth century, many Russian towns and monasteries gained impressive new new brick walls similar to those in Rostov. The Muscovite skill for building with large, well-fired bricks reached unprecedented levels, as is demonstrated in Kazan's Siuiumbeki Tower. Although named after a Tatar princess of the time of Ivan the Terrible, the structure was probably built as a watchtower in the late seventeenth century by a master from Moscow. It was during this period (1660s-1680s) that the towers of the Moscow Kremlin gained their tiered superstructures, often with spires, that so distinguish them; and the Borovitsk Tower (built in 1490 by Pietro Antonio Solari, with receding superstructure added in 1666–1680s) seems in particular to have served as a model for Kazan tower. The engineering of the Kazan tower (58 meters in height) depended on the quality of the brick and on a base whose thickness is comparable to that of the Bell Tower of Ivan the Great. In 1913 the Siuiumbeki Tower served as the inspiration for Aleksei Shchusev's design of the Kazan Railway Station in Moscow.

MONASTERY OF ST. NICHOLAS AT VIAZHISHCHE. NEAR NOVGOROD

The flourishing of monastery construction in that late seventeenth century produced not only large walled compounds, but also compact, richly-decorated ensembles such as the Monastery of St. Nicholas at Viazhishche, twelve kilometers to the northwest of Novgorod. The monastery Cathedral of St. Nicholas, rebuilt in 1681–85 by the conservative Metropolitan Kornily of Novgorod, follows the traditional four-piered design, with five cupolas and a multi-gabled roof line typical of Novgorod churches. The most complex part of its form is the ascending entrance gallery, culminating in a single zakomara gable and flanked by two towers with pyramidal roofs.

By 1694 the energetic abbot of the monastery, Bogolep Sablin, had initiated a new refectory and church adjacent to the cathedral. In contrast to the austerely monumental design used for the main monastic churches, the accepted practice for refec-

Rostov   Gate Church of St. John the Divine. Interior.

Kazan   Siuiumbeki Tower, kremlin. Late 17th century. Southeast view.

Novgorod   Cathedral, Monastery of St. Nicholas at Viazhishche. 1681–85. Northwest view.

Novgorod   Refectory Church of St. John the Divine, Monastery of St. Nicholas at
Viazhishche. 1694–1704. Southeast view.

tory churches in the seventeenth century involved greater ornamentation, a reflection of their function as centers of monastic conviviality. Such is the case with the
refectory Church of St. John the Divine, whose great length culminates in the west
with a bell tower (the last element to be completed, in 1704) and in the east with a
two-story structure containing churches dedicated to St. John the Divine (below),
and to the Ascension (above). The entire length is marked with two strips of ornamental tiles on a green base, depicting primarily floral patterns but also containing
mythological beasts (unicorn, two-headed eagle) and iconographic motifs. The
church and bell tower have additional strips decorating their greater height, and the
church in particular has elaborate ceramic window surrounds rivaled in scale and
magnificence only by Yaroslavl churches such as John the Baptist at Tolchkovo.

REFECTORY CHURCH OF ST. SERGIUS, TRINITY-ST. SERGIUS
MONASTERY. SERGIEV POSAD

The most notable example of refectory architecture during the flourishing of
monastery construction in the late seventeenth century is the St. Sergius Church,
built in 1686–92 with a wealth of facade detail that epitomizes late Muscovite ornamentalism. The peculiarly Russian institution of a refectory (or monastic dining
hall and kitchen) with attached stone church had first appeared in the Kremlin
Chudov Monastery at the end of the fifteenth century. Thereafter, the arrangement
spread to several major monasteries and convents, including the Trinity-St.

Sergiev Posad   Refectory Church of St. Sergius, Trinity-St. Sergius Monastery. 1686–92.
North view.

Sergius Monastery, whose earlier refectory dated from the 1560s, with a church
added in 1621. The Church of St. Sergius, 85 meters in length (including the exterior elevated terrace), was comprised of the main hall 34 meters long without a
central column, and a two-story church with domical vault. The interior is decorated with wall paintings and gilded ornament. The exterior, covered with polychrome diamond rustication, has elaborate window surrounds with molded
columns that were first introduced in 1682 with the widening of the windows of
the Faceted Chambers in the Moscow Kremlin.

NOVODEVICHY CONVENT. MOSCOW

Of all Moscow's monastic institutions, none prospered more openly during the
seventeenth century than the Novodevichy (New Virgin) Convent. A major building campaign was supported by the Tsarevna Sophia during her regency
(1682–1689). She was assisted in this endeavor by her main advisor Prince Vasily
Golitsyn, an architectural innovator interested in western forms and willing to
implement them on an imposing scale. The clearest example of the palatial, secular orientation of the style is the refectory Church of the Dormition (1685–1687),
with a complex entablature and attached columns framing the bays and window
surrounds. More idiosyncratic in design, is the brilliant Church of the
Transfiguration, over the north gates (1687–1689). The gilded five domes and
crosses rise above a cornice of zakomary with the scallop shell motif. This orna-

Moscow   Gate Church of the Transfiguration, Novodevichy Convent. 1687–89. South view.

ment, and the complementary window surrounds, summarize the essence of "Moscow Baroque" style, although other churches display it in greater structural and decorative complexity. The south gate Church of the Intercession (1683–1688) is more modest in its decorative detail but has the unusual design of three towers of ascending octagons surmounted with gilded cupolas. Both of the gate churches have terraces over the gates and at the base of the church proper, thus creating a platform for the jeweled structures above.

ST. JOSEPH-VOLOKOLAMSK MONASTERY.
NEAR VOLOKOLAMSK

One of the most successful contemporary restoration efforts in Russia is the Joseph-Volokolamsk Monastery at the village of Teriaevo, near Volokolamsk. The monastery was founded in 1479 by Joseph Volotsky, a prominent cleric who vigorously defended the prerogatives of the church and its monasteries in accumulating wealth. During the latter half of the seventeenth century a major campaign to rebuild and expand the monastery resulted in the magnificent ensemble that exists today. Until the Second World War a large octagonal bell tower rose above the middle of the Joseph-Volokolamsk Monastery, but in the fall of 1941 this potential observation tower was demolished by the retreating Soviet army with little damage to the adjacent Cathedral.

Teriaevo (near Volokolamsk)   Cathedral of the Dormition, Joseph-Volokolamsk Monastery. 1690s. Southwest view.

The centerpiece of the ensemble is the Cathedral of the Dormition, rebuilt in 1688–92 with the support of masters from the Moscow Kremlin. Although designed in the typical cuboid form, the cathedral is notable for its height and its ornamental bands of ceramic tiles on the "peacock feather" motif. The interior of the Dormition Cathedral, with frescoes and a late seventeenth-century iconostasis, has survived relatively well, despite a number of missing icons. The four columns at the crossing soar to the main drum and dome, whose narrow windows flood the central space with light, just as the corner bays are illuminated by the four flanking drums.

CATHEDRAL OF THE DORMITION. RIAZAN

Riazan is one of the oldest cities to the south of Moscow, and during the seventeenth century it was one of the most important. In 1684 work began on a rebuilding of its main cathedral, dedicated to the Dormition, but the completed walls collapsed in 1692. The project was then entrusted to the architect Yakov Bukhvostov, who also had much trouble with the foundations and the roof vaulting for the immense structure. The interior plan contains four massive columns for the central and west bays, and two extended piers at the east bay and iconostasis.

Teriaevo   Cathedral of the Dormition, Joseph-Volokolamsk Monastery. Interior.

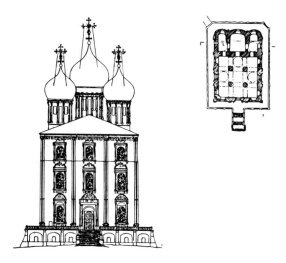

Riazan   Dormition Cathedral. Elevation, plan.

Over forty meters in height, with five large drums and cupolas as well as extensive window space, the structure is indeed precariously balanced on Bukhvostov's system of cellar vaults, which also provide a terrace platform for the cathedral.

Like its predecessor by Fioravanti in the Kremlin, the Riazan Dormition Cathedral resembles a great three-story hall. Its roofline was designed as a horizonal dentilated cornice, and the tall windows were framed with carved limestone columns and pediments. The some 5,000 blocks comprising the limestone details were standardized, thus enabling the architect to complete the structure by 1699, a relatively short period in view of the complexity of the project and Bukhvostov's ongoing work elsewhere. To a degree unequalled in late Muscovite architecture, the window surrounds and the paired brick columns (painted white) that segment

Riazan   Cathedral of the Dormition (1693–1702) with belltower (1789–97). Northwest view.

the brick facades provide a secular, palatial ambience to one of the largest churches of the seventeenth century—larger, in fact, than Moscow's Dormition Cathedral.

CHURCH OF THE INTERCESSION AT FILI. MOSCOW

The first masterpiece of the "Naryshkin Baroque" style is the Church of the Intercession at Fili, built in 1690–1693 by the boiar Lev Naryshkin, uncle of Peter I. Its plan is both decorative and tightly organized: a cube with four projecting lobes, of which the east and west are elongated. All projections but the east (apsidal) have a staircase with balustrade descending from the gallery that encircles the structure. The festive, ceremonial function of this design of steps, in two landings with a right-angle turn, had been explored at the Ascension Church at Kolomenskoe, and is applied with the decorative panoply of the Naryshkin style, which here consists of cornice crests ("combs") and attached columns without ornamental carving on the shafts. The distinctive quality of church, emphasized by the application of decorative detail, is the handling of proportion and structural development, from the raised gallery—which reinforces the plasticity of the projecting lobes, each with its own gilded cupola—to the cupola above the central tower and belfry. Despite the stylistic distance that separates the Fili church from contemporary European architecture, its unknown architect possessed an unerring sense of an ordered tectonic system relating all parts to a harmonious whole.

Moscow   Church of the Intercession at Fili.

Moscow Church of the Intercession at Fili. 1690-93. South View.

The luxuriously outfitted but small interior, with carved iconostasis, is essentially a cylinder, linked at the base of the main cupola with iron tie rods.

CHURCH OF THE ICON OF THE SIGN AT DUBROVITSY. PODOLSK

The ultimate saturation point of the Naryshkin style was reached in the Church of the Icon of the Sign on the estate of Dubrovitsy (near Podolsk, to the west of Moscow). Commissioned in 1690 by Boris Golitsyn, tutor of Peter I, the basic struc-

Moscow   Church of the Intercession at Fili. Interior.

ture was completed in 1697, yet the church was consecrated only in 1704, in the presence of Tsar Peter. The identity of its builders and the sculptors of its profuse statuary has been the subject of much speculation, yet all hypotheses have so far proved untenable. Whatever the resolution to that question, the church spans the most productive years of the tiered style, and is a catalog of its experiments in structure and in the decorative arts—both interior and exterior. In plan the Dubrovitsy church has a symmetrical configuration whose tower rises directly from the four lobes of the first tier—apparently what Bukhvostov had intended at Ubory. Thus it is, along with the church at Fili, one of the early examples of the centralized plan.

CHURCH OF THE ARCHANGEL GABRIEL (MENSHIKOV TOWER). MOSCOW

The clearest statement of the vertical in Moscow church architecture was also the first to proclaim the new order of Petrine architecture. The Church of the Archangel Gabriel, built in 1701–1707 on the city estate of Peter the Great's assistant Alexander Menshikov, is rectangular in plan, with a semicircular gable at the center of each facade. The festive nature of the church is expressed in its use of a major Corinthian order for the pilasters and fluted columns that frame the center bay and portal, as well as stucco festoons and cherubim. The main entrance on the west front is still more massively framed by pylons, volutes, and columns, with a stucco relief of the Ascension of Christ swathed in billowing clouds above the portal.

Podolsk   Church of the Icon of the Sign at Dubrovitsy. 1690-97; 1704. Southeast view.

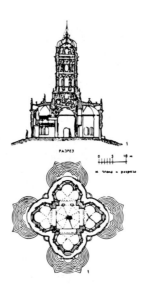

Podolsk   Church of the Icon of the Sign at Dubrovitsy. Section, plan.

   The initial form of the church, with a wooden, metal-sheathed spire reaching a height of 81 meters, consisted of three octagonal tiers above the rectangular base, thus showing a continuity with the Naryshkin baroque towers. The main octagon originally supported statues of archangels. The general design of the edifice is attributed to Ivan Zarudny, but it is known that project also involved Italian architects and sculptors. The brickwork was implemented by a team of masons from Yaroslavl and Kostroma, both centers of brick production and craftsmanship. After the building of Petersburg began in earnest, however, Menshikov resettled in the northern capital in 1710, and interior work on the church proceeded slowly. A lightning strike and fire in 1723 not only toppled the wooden spire but destroyed the supports for an English chiming clock and 50 bells, all of which plunged below, taking with them much of the vaulting and interior decoration. The main structure was not rebuilt until 1773–1779, at which time the uppermost octagonal tier was replaced with an elongated decorative cupola and the facades were stuccoed.

Moscow Church of the Archangel Gabriel (Menshikov Tower). 1701–07. South view.

8. EIGHTEENTH CENTURY BAROQUE

CATHEDRAL OF SAINTS PETER AND PAUL. ST. PETERSBURG

Trezzini's design of the Cathedral of Saints Peter and Paul represents a radical departure from traditional Russian church architecture, based on a centralized, cross-domed plan. Here Trezzini created an elongated rectangular structure, whose modest baroque dome, on the eastern end, is subordinate to the tower and spire placed over the west entrance. Indeed, the tower was the main focus of Peter's interest, and had priority over the rest of the structure, which was not completed until 1732. Rapid construction of the tower not only created a platform from which Peter could, in his obsessive way, survey construction progress over the entire area, but it also provided a frame for the carillon, with chiming clock, that he had commissioned in Holland. By 1717 Trezzini had completed the basic structure of the tower (the spire was assembled in 1720), and in 1720 the carillon was installed. By 1723 the spire, gilded and surmounted with an angel holding a cross, reached a height of 112 meters, which exceeded the bell tower of Ivan the Great by 32 meters.

The spire, like the body of the cathedral, resembles the seventeenth-century Baroque architecture of northern Europe, with its combination of large volutes bracing the lower tiers of the tower and elements of classical entablature in the segmentation of the ascending levels. The large windows that mark the length of the church are in articulation and design unprecedented in Russian church architecture, and provide ample illumination for the banners and other imperial regalia that mark the interior. It is not clear whether this great hall was originally intended to serve as a burial place for the Romanov tsars; but with the death of Peter the Great (whose funeral was held in a temporary wooden church erected within the walls of the uncompleted cathedral), this function was assumed from the Archangel Cathedral in the Kremlin.

The interior of the cathedral, divided by faux marbre piers with gilded corinthian capitals into three aisles, is decorated with pastel trompe l'oeil architectural detail that seems to extend the space of the vaulting. The upper part of the walls display panels on religious themes, which although done in the Western manner, were painted by a collective of Russian artists. The centerpiece of the interior, however, is the gilded iconostasis beneath the dome in the eastern end of the church. Its design,

St. Petersburg   Cathedral of Sts. Peter and Paul, Peter-Paul Fortress. 1712–32. Southwest view.

St. Petersburg   Cathedral of Sts. Peter and Paul, Peter-Paul Fortress. Interior.

by Ivan Zarudny, bears a much closer resemblance to the triumphal arches erected to celebrate events of state—particularly Peter's victories—than to the elaborate icon screens of the late seventeenth century. Yet the craftsmanship of the latter was readily adaptable to the demands of the Baroque style, of which this iconostasis is a most accomplished example. The frame, with allegorical figures, trumpeting angels, cherubim, twisted columns and broken pediments surrounding a central icon of the Ascension, was carved between 1722 and 1726 by master craftsmen in Moscow, and assembled in the cathedral in 1727. It is now assumed that the icons were painted on site by the Moscow painter Andrei Pospelov and his assistants; but whatever the precise details of its assembly, the style of the painting is Western.

BUILDING OF THE TWELVE COLLEGES. ST. PETERSBURG

The last of Domenico Trezzini's extant major projects, the Building of the Twelve Colleges contained the offices of the ten state ministries ("colleges"), as well as the Senate (the highest judicial body) and the Holy Synod—all administrative units devised by Peter, with the advice of Gottfried Leibniz, in an attempt to base the Russian bureaucracy on modern Western principles of organization. Emblematic of the rationalist ideology of Peter's reforms, the building, 383 meters in length, also exemplifies of the era's experimentation with construction methods—organized in theory but chaotic in practice. According to Peter's instructions of 1723, the various

St. Petersburg   Building of the Twelve Colleges. 1722–41

departments were to be joined in a single row, and each was to have its own, uniform roof, with interior rooms arranged to the needs of each department. Peter, however, reopened the competition for the facade design; and while Trezzini's general concept was retained, much of the detail of the upper two floors is now attributed to Theodor Schwertfeger. Intended to give both flexibility and uniform construction tasks to each of the departments, the system created confusion in the delivery of materials and the coordination of schedules. After Trezzini's death in 1734, the project continued until its completion in 1741 under the direction of his son-in-law Giuseppe Trezzini, who constructed a gallery along the entire length of the "back," or west, facade.

KUNSTKAMMER. ST. PETERSBURG

Of the extant Petrine monuments on Vasilevsky Island, the most visible is the Kunstkammer, or Chamber of Curiosities, the first of Petersburg's academic institutions devoted to the diffusion of scientific knowledge. Situated on the Neva embankment within the tip of Vasilevsky Island (near the future Twelve Colleges), the structure was designed by the Swiss-German architect Georg-Johann Mattarnovy, who had arrived in Petersburg in 1714 on the recommendation of the renowned Prussian architect Andreas Schlüter, himself hired by Peter the previous year as chief architect of the city. (Neither withstood the rigors of Petersburg:

St. Petersburg   Kunstkammer. 1718–34

Schlüter died several months after his arrival, and Mattarnovy died in 1719.) Although begun in 1718, the Kunstkammer was not completed until 1734, by which time a succession of architects, including Gaetano Chiaveri and Mikhail Zemtsov, had modified Mattarnovy's original design, with its florid Baroque pediments and statuary flanking the central tower. Nonetheless, the basic outlines remain and are marked by the extensive use of white trim on a pastel stuccoed facade—a device common to the work of Trezzini and Schwertfeger.

The symbolic significance of the Kunstkammer as a center of learning is expressed in the central tower, culminating in a polygonal lantern and globe representing Peter's interest in science and its applications for a new age of exploration in Russia. The tower design has been compared with that of Schlüter's Münzthurm in Berlin, and it is not improbable that Mattarnovy, Schlüter's protégé, would have had access to the master's sketches in Petersburg. On the interior the tower housed a circular anatomy theater and an observatory—the first in Russia. On either side of the tower extended the library and museum collection, which were in turn flanked by wings containing office space. The viability of this logical design is attested by the continuing function of the building as an ethnographic institute, with library and much of the original collection acquired by Peter. Within the context of Vasilevsky Island the Kunstkammer tower not only provides a vertical dominant within the succession of classical facades along the island's embankment, but also mediates between the spires of the Peter-Paul Cathedral and, on the south bank of the Neva, the Admiralty.

MENSHIKOV PALACE. ST. PETERSBURG

Early palace architecture in St. Petersburg only rarely achieved a grand scale, such as the residence of Aleksandr Menshikov on Vasilevsky Island. Located on the Neva, with a garden extending into the center of the island, the masonry palace was begun in 1710 to a design by Giovanni Mario Fontana and completed in the

St. Petersburg   Menshikov Palace. 1710–20s

early 1720s—with attached wings converting much of the garden into a court-yard—by Gottfried Johann Schädel. Menshikov and his family were summarily evicted from the palace following his downfall in 1727, during the reign of Peter II, and in 1732 the residence was converted to use as a military institute. Its steeply-pitched mansard roof with flanking towers was removed, as was a row of allegorical statues over the entrance. A recent restoration has uncovered much of the original decorative work on the interior, including the lavish use of Dutch tiles, carved paneling, extensive stucco ornament, and several ceiling paintings. The pilaster capitals on the second level of the main facade are among the early examples of the use of the composite order in Russia, and indicate an interest in reproducing elements of the order system in the new architecture.

MAIN PALACE. PETERHOF

The greatest palace builder of the Baroque era in Russia was Bartolomeo Francesco Rastrelli. Although he had designed a number of palaces in the 1730s, his accession to rococo magnificence began in 1745 with a commission to rebuild the main palace at Peterhof. Although basic structural work was completed in 1752, the interior decoration continued until 1755, and remodeling began almost immediately thereafter. His design adhered to the early Baroque style of the first Peterhof palace (by Le Blond), particularly the central structure, which remained close to its original form on the exterior and also preserved certain rooms associated with

Peterhof　Main Palace. 1745–55

Peter the Great. The Petrine style is also evident in the mansard roof of both the central part and the end pavilions, which were considerably expanded by Rastrelli. The use of pilasters and rusticated quoins—virtually the only ornamental features of the stuccoed facade—is restrained in comparison with the decoration of Rastrelli's later works, yet entirely appropriate for the early Baroque.

The late Baroque, however, is evident in the designs for the two end pavilions: the court church and the Imperial Insignia pavilion, so-named for the two-headed eagle placed above the cupola. The cupolas of the pavilions rest on pyramidal projections whose edges are outlined with gilded festoons. The court church suggests a Baroque reinterpretation of traditional Russian forms. The link was all the clearer in the original pentacupolar design of the church, whose corner cupolas are one of the earliest examples of the return of that form in post-Petrine architecture. The gilded cupolas of both pavilions not only provide definition of the extent of the structure, but also complement the brilliant yellow of the facade, highlighted by white trim.

The plan of the palace reflected the relatively informality of what was considered primarily a summer residence on the gulf. The main entrance and stairway are situated to the side of the palace, in the west wing (extending into the Upper Park) and lead directly to the grand state rooms: the Ballroom, the Chesme Hall (remodeled during the reign of Catherine II), and the Great Throne Hall—perpendicular to the west wing and extending for almost a quarter of the main facade. In the center is a clusters of salons or "apartments" which lead to two parallel enfilades connecting a series of dining rooms, studies, and other state rooms. Beyond this core structure, one-story galleries led to the palace church beyond the east wing, and the Imperial Insignia pavilion to the west.

The creation of the luxuriant interior at Peterhof demanded not only a large workforce of craftsmen but also the subsequent collaboration of the architect Vallin de la Mothe in the 1760s. In the 1770s Georg Veldten redid much of the interior to suit Catherine's tastes, but a number of the major rooms, such as the Great Hall retained much of Rastrelli's work. In addition to the characteristic use of plaster ornament, gilded rococo details, and mirrors, the interior also contained ceiling paintings on allegorical themes, most notably by Bartolomeo Tarsia in the Portrait Hall and the Ballroom, and a series of painted oval portraits by Giuseppe Valeriani in the Ballroom. After their almost total destruction during World War II, many of the rooms have been reconstructed with much of their interior decoration.

CATHERINE PALACE. TSARSKOE SELO

In 1752 Rastrelli, who as Chief Architect to the court was in charge of all palace construction, took over direct control of work at Tsarskoe Selo with the purpose of creating a palace on a scale befitting a major European power. To this end Rastrelli demolished much of a just-completed rebuilding of the palace and added a third story to the main structure, which was extended the full length of the palace. The initial elegant design appropriate to a country palace, with galleries and an orangery, became a display of imperial wealth on an unprecedented scale. With thousands of laborers and 400 masons from Yaroslavl, whose brick churches had been the glory of seventeenth-century Russia, Rastrelli oversaw the building and

Tsarskoe Selo Catherine Palace. 1752–60s

rebuilding of the palace in a process that Catherine the Great called "Penelope's labor." The frequent revision and expansion of the palace's plans seems to have been devoid of any constraints usually imposed on architects by the realities of construction—most notably, expense.

The removal during Catherine's reign of the gilt from much of the exterior impedes an immediate impression of the effect this enormous mass must have produced in Elizabeth's time: gilded atlantes supporting white columns against a turquoise background, surmounted by a golden balustrade—decorated with golden vases and statuary—and culminating in the silver hue of a sheet-iron roof. The palace is over 325 meters in length, and the facade is perhaps best appreciated in fragments, as seen through clearings in the park or from the main palace gates. From this perspective the palace, with or without gilt, reveals Rastrelli's genius for color and form. Above the rusticated ground floor, with its arcade of French windows separated by atlantes, the building is marked by white attached columns that give the azure facade a depth unknown in his earlier palaces. Despite the symmetry of the facade, its culminating point is not the central structure, but rather the pentacupolar church that anchors the east wing of the palace. The Baroque articulation of the gilded cupolas shows an clear resemblance to his design for the Church of St. Andrew in Kiev (1748–1762), yet it also anticipates Rastrelli's union of Baroque and Russian Orthodox church architecture at the Smolnyi Convent.

The resolution of the Catherine Palace in favor of its end point (a corresponding domed pavilion on the west end was later modified during the reign of Catherine II) suits the horizontal essence of the structure. This principle was reaffirmed in Rastrelli's plan for the interior, whose main entrance was from the west wing. From that point two parallel enfilades extended the entire length of the palace without the interruption of a central cluster of rooms. The later central vestibule and grand stairway, built for Catherine II by Charles Cameron in 1780 and remodeled in 1860 by Ippolit Monighetti, established a mid point that allows one to proceed to either half of the enfilade; yet the sense of one integral space in the original plan is undiminished.

At Tsarskoe Selo, Rastrelli's fondness for placing the main stairway to the side of the structure enabled the design of a series of antechambers leading to the aptly named Great Hall, 48 meters in length, whose arcades of French windows are interspersed with mirrors and rococo gilt decoration. The combination of natural light and mirrored reflection dissolves the boundaries of the room, enormous allegorical ceiling painting (of Russia partaking the bounties of civilization, executed in 1753 by Valeriani) would otherwise weigh heavily on the space, despite its height. It must be emphasized that the palace interior at Tsarskoe Selo, like that at Peterhof, is a scrupulous reconstruction, itself a heroic task that began almost immediately after World War II, and continues to this day.

STROGANOV PALACE. ST. PETERSBURG

Rastrelli's greatest palace for a private individual survived relatively intact, as did the fortunes of the Stroganovs who commissioned it and remained there until 1917. Not only did the Stroganov clan possess fabulous wealth, dating to the fifteenth century and greatly expanded in the sixteenth and seventeenth centuries

St. Petersburg Stroganov Palace. 1752–54

with the exploitation of salt mines and foundries in the Urals, but they were also related by marriage to Empress Elizabeth, who made available Rastrelli's services. Baron Sergei Stroganov had ample means to pay for the construction of his palace, which was completed in slightly over two years, from 1752 to 1754. Although small in comparison with the imperial palaces, the Stroganov residence displays a flawless command of the relation between structure and decoration, particularly in the articulation of the window surrounds. They are a marvel of ingenuity on both the Nevsky Prospekt and Moika Canal facades, as well as on the interior courtyard. Due to a considerable rise in the street level along the Nevsky facade, the proportions of the structure seem lower than in the original design.

In plan the Stroganov Palace is constructed on the perimeter of its lot, bounded by Nevsky Prospekt and the Moika (the building code for the prospekt required construction flush with the street line). In addition Stroganov himself stipulated that the Moika facade should be as imposing as that facing the prospekt, and Rastrelli created a complex grouping of attached columns, cornice, and pediment on the piano nobile overlooking the canal. Because of the unusual perimeter design, however, the design of the interior courtyard also assumed a special importance. Upon entering from Nevsky Prospekt through the large wooden gates—decorated with Rastrelli's signature Baroque lion masks—one is in the midst of a protected space, which, although not as grand as either of the street facades, contains some of his most ingenious stucco decorative work.

The frequent, emphatic references to Italian work and the Italian manner suggest that the northern European Baroque, which had manifold connections to Italian architecture, was being supplanted in Russia by a more direct perception of

Italy as a source of architectural style and as an ultimate authority in the definition of proper architecture. In the early 1790s much of the Baroque interior of the palace was destroyed by fire. The Stroganovs were, however, fortunate to have the rooms redesigned by one of the greatest Russian architects, their own freed serf Andrei Voronikhin.

WINTER PALACE. ST. PETERSBURG

Discussions for the creation of a new, fourth, Winter Palace for Empress Elizabeth began in the early 1750s, and by 1753 Bartolomeo Francesco Rastrelli had submitted the final variant of his plan. He operated under constraints similar to those imposed at Peterhof and Tsarskoe Selo: to incorporate a large existing structure (in this case Rastrelli's own Third Winter Palace) into the design of a still larger work, staggering in both size and cost. As construction proceeded during 1754, Rastrelli concluded that the new palace would involve not simply an expansion of the old, but would have to be built over its foundations, thus necessitating the razing of the previous structure.

The plan of the Winter Palace resembles, albeit on a far greater scale, the perimeter concept of the Stroganov Palace, with a quadrilateral interior courtyard decorated in a manner similar to the outer walls. The exterior facades of the new imperial palace—three of which are turned toward great public spaces—can only be compared to those of the Catherine Palace at Tsarskoe Selo. On the river facade the palace presents from a distance an uninterrupted horizontal sweep of over 200 meters, while the Palace Square facade is marked in the center by the three arches of the main courtyard entrance. The facade overlooking the Admiralty is the one area of the structure that contains substantial elements of the previous palace walls; and the decorative detailing of its central part of the facade, flanked by two wings, reflects the earlier mannerisms of Rastrelli's style.

Although symmetry reigns in the articulation of the facades, each has its own form in the design of pediments and the spacing of attached columns, whose distribution provides an insistent rhythm to the horizontal expanse. The 250 columns segment some 700 windows (not including those of the interior court), whose surrounds are decorated in 20 different patterns reflecting the array of ornamental motifs—including lion masks and other grotesque figures—accumulated by Rastrelli over a period of three decades. The three main floors of the Winter Palace are situated over a basement level, whose semicircular window surrounds establish an arcade effect that is followed in the tiers of windows above. The horizontal dimensions of the palace are emphasized by a string course separating the two upper floors from the first, and by the complex profile of the cornice, above which is a balustrade supporting 176 large ornamental vases and allegorical statues.

CATHEDRAL OF THE RESURRECTION, SMOLNY CONVENT. ST. PETERSBURG

The culmination of Rastrelli's work occurred with the design of the Cathedral of the Resurrection at the Resurrection Newmaiden Convent—commonly known as the Smolny (from the Russian for "tar") because of its location near the site where tar

St. Petersburg Winter Palace. 1754–64

St. Petersburg   Cathedral of the Resurrection, Smolny Convent. 1748–60s. West view.

had been stored for Peter's navy. Elizabeth wished to found not only a convent but also an institute for the education of young noblewomen. Work on the foundations for the cathedral and the conventual buildings began in 1748, as shifts of soldiers (as many as 2,000) dug trenches and drove some 50,000 four- and twelve-meter piles into the marshy soil along the Neva. The large square perimeter of the convent contained enclosed galleries linking the living and administrative quarters, as well as churches placed at the four corners. The center of the compound was occupied by the cathedral, which the empress specified to be built along the lines of the Cathedral of the Dormition in the Moscow Kremlin: a cross-domed plan with five cupolas. The reign of Elizabeth thus marks the resurgence of the traditional Russian Orthodox plan, modified by Western influence. In addition, the entrance to the convent was to support a colossal bell tower constructed with ascending tiers derived from the bell tower of Ivan the Great, but at least twice its height.

Construction proceeded slowly after Elizabeth's approval in 1749 of the plan submitted by Rastrelli, but by 1760 the exterior of the cathedral had assumed its final shape. After Elizabeth's death at the end of 1761, the bell tower was eliminated from the plan. The convent was completed only in 1764 under the direction of Georg Friedrich Veldten, and the cathedral interior was not finished until the 1830s, in a neoclassical style by Vasily Stasov that bears little relation to Rastrelli's intention.

Rastrelli's design of the cathedral exterior, however, is relatively intact and reveals the ingenuity with which he fused Eastern and Western elements. The four subsidiary cupolas, placed on double-tiered towers, are grouped around a central dome supporting the fifth cupola, in a pattern derived from the Russian pentacupolar church; yet their placement and design, as well as the form of the ribbed dome, are reminiscent rather of Borromini and the seventeenth-century Roman baroque. Nonetheless, the tightly integrated, monolithic mass of the central and subsidiary domes is related to two of the greatest of medieval Russian monuments—the Kremlin Dormition Cathedral and the Novgorod St. Sophia. The vertical thrust of the cathedral is echoed by the four corner chapels, whose elongated single domes appear from a distance to be extensions of the main structure.

When viewed from the front, the corners of the successive planes that comprise the west facade—marked by pilasters and clusters of columns—advance toward the entrance portal and provide a suitably imposing base for the great dome, which rises to a height of almost 100 meters. The side facades present a more even, unified plane, with only a portal to mark the center of the luxuriant plaster decoration of the facade. As usual for the design of baroque churches in Petersburg, the apse is not given a major structural role, and is only slightly visible as a rectangular projection on the east facade. Also characteristic of Baroque architecture in Russia is the use of color to delineate the building's structural and decorative elements—in this case white on a pastel-blue stucco facade.

CATHEDRAL OF ST. NICHOLAS. ST. PETERSBURG

The one Baroque church in Petersburg to rival Rastrelli's design at Smolnyi is the Cathedral of St. Nicholas, built in 1753–1762 by Savva Chevakinsky, whose previous accomplishments had included extensive work on the imperial estates. The

St. Petersburg   Cathedral of St. Nicholas. 1753–62. North view.

location of this azure form, with white trim and golden domes, is near the intersection of the Catherine and Kriukov Canals. Although the trees of the surrounding plaza obscure the boundaries of the building, its salient features are
nonetheless evident. The design of the cathedral combines a rigorous and finely
calculated symmetry with an assured handling of profuse baroque decoration. Its
plan can be classified as cruciform, with a single bay inserted within each corner
of the cross. Although there are variations in the ornamental work on the separate

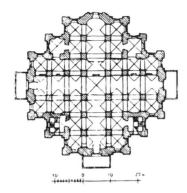

St. Petersburg Cathedral of St. Nicholas. Plan.

facades—particularly the east, or apsidal facade—the north, south and west are strongly centered by the triple corinthian columns that frame the portal. These columns lead to a semi-circular pediment with elaborate stucco decorative work that seems to exhaust the possibilities of cherubic faces. Indeed, the entablature of the main structure approaches that of the classical system of orders, broken by bursts of cherubim on the capitals and by botanical ornament instead of triglyphs. Chevakinsky's design emphasizes the horizontal, in contrast to the verticality of the cathedral at Smolnyi. Its superbly proportioned central dome does not dominate the four widely-spaced subsidiary domes, which gain spatial autonomy at the corners of the structure (they rest on the four "inserted" bays within the arms of the cruciform plan).

On the interior, the portals give access to a ground-level "winter" church, above which is the main church, well lit and of spacious proportions. It is reached by stairways in the two west corner bays, each of which is illuminated by its cupola drum. Chevakinsky calculated the relation between structure, function, and decoration as skillfully as any medieval Russian master; and he had the fortune, denied Rastrelli at Smolnyi, to implement his own design for the interior, whose centerpiece is a wooden iconostasis, intricately carved and decorated with Baroque and classical elements.

Chevakinsky's combination of tradition and innovation are perhaps most effectively stated in the cathedral's splendid bell tower. Since the seventeenth century, bell towers were usually attached to the west structure of Russian churches, yet the traditional separate bell tower was still viable. Chevakinsky placed a free-standing tower on a direct axis with the west entrance of his cathedral, but at a distance of some 30 meters. Poised over the Kriukov Canal, the tower not only provides the vertical dominant that is muted in the structure itself, but also marks the west facade and the main entrance to the cathedral.

9. NEOCLASSICISM

ACADEMY OF ARTS. ST. PETERSBURG

When compared with the work of Rastrelli, whose Winter Palace had only recently been completed, Kokorinov and Vallin de la Mothe's design for the Academy of Arts is the essence of simplicity. Without elaborate statuary or plaster ornamentation, the main facade of the three-story building is marked by tetrastyle Tuscan porticos on either end and, in the center, a projecting pediment with two supporting columns on each side of a large window on the main level. This five-part division of a neoclassical facade, with an advanced central pediment, had been established by Le Vau, Perrault, and Le Brun on the East front of the Louvre. Unlike the French prototype, however, the Academy of Arts uses the more modest pilasters, rather than a colonnade, to defined the middle sections. Furthermore, the walls are not of natural stone, but of stuccoed brick, rusticated on the ground floor.

Despite delays in completing the building (much of which remained unfurnished until 1810), the academy continued to function in parts of the enormous structure (125 x 140 meters), rivaled in size only by the Winter Palace. The plan included a series of self-enclosed, autonomous units organized around four rectangular courtyards, which are themselves attached to a great circular courtyard in the center of the structure. Not only are the facades regulated by a strict symmetry, but the plan itself represents an elaborate exercise in geometrical form.

Although certain baroque features remain, such as the curved projection of the central pediment, the Academy of Arts building marks a clear division between the baroque and the neoclassical. Its cornice displays one of the earliest Russian uses of a proper entablature, above which is a simple attic with no ornamentation—both features signaling the advance of neoclasscism. And the large wooden model of the structure played a role in the propagation of the style among the academy's students.

NEW HOLLAND. ST. PETERSBURG

The most monumental, and arguably the strongest, of Vallin de la Mothe's designs is the arch for New Holland, a complex of canals, basins, and wooden warehouses originally built by Ivan Korobov in 1732–1740 to store lumber for the navy. In 1765

St. Petersburg   Academy of Arts. 1765–89

Savva Chevakinsky began to rebuild the warehouses in brick, but the design for the exterior facades and the major gateway to the complex was given to Vallin de la Mothe. The unstuccoed brick facades (those that were completed before the project was halted in the 1780s) are detailed without decoration as a three-story monolithic arcade that is itself an architectural statement of geometry and mass.

The magnificent arch, large enough for a boat to enter through the canal leading to a turning basin, is framed by paired Tuscan columns of gray granite supporting the projecting entablature. Within the brick facade behind each pair of columns is an arched niche, above which is a simple medallion. They are sepa-

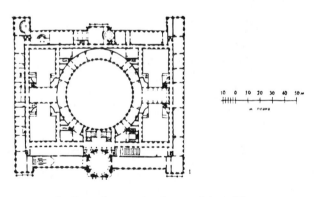

St. Petersburg   Academy of Arts. Plan.

St. Petersburg   New Holland. 1765–80s

rated by a stone cornice that leads to the capital of a smaller Tuscan column on each side of the entrance arch. Thus the major and minor orders are closely linked. The entryway, with its highly pitched arch, uses open space to define the harmony of structural proportions. Above and on either side of the arch is an abstracted festoon, also of stone; and the central part culminates in a continuation of the doric entablature.

MARBLE PALACE. ST. PETERSBURG

Remarkably little is known of the biography of Antonio Rinaldi (1710?–1794) before his arrival in Petersburg in 1754. He was a student of Luigi Vanvitelli, and presumably assisted the latter in the construction of the Royal Palace at Caserta, begun in 1751. The influence of that Neapolitan masterpiece—the last of the great Baroque palaces of Italy—appears in the palaces Rinaldi designed in Petersburg and its suburbs, with their combination of luxuriant decoration and austere monumentality.

Rinaldi's sensitivity to the shades of natural stone culminated in the building subsequently known as the Marble Palace. Commissioned by Catherine for her favorite Grigory Orlov, the palace was begun in 1768; but the interior was not completed until 1785, by which time Catherine had repurchased it from the surviving Orlov brothers. Like the Winter Palace, it is visually divided into two levels

St. Petersburg   Marble Palace. 1768–85

culminating in a cornice and attic. The ground floor, of rough-grained red Finnish granite, forms a sharp contrast to the subtle coloration of the two upper floors, with gray granite walls and architectural details in several varieties of marble: polished pink Karelian marble for the two-story Corinthian pilasters that provide both vertical and horizontal definition to the upper level; capitals and festoons (between the second and third floors) of white Urals marble; veined bluish gray marble from the Urals for panels beneath the festoons; Karelian marble for the attic frieze, above which are ornamental urns of Reval dolomite.

The facades of the Marble Palace are designed with a rigorous symmetry, yet the trapezoidal plan of the structure necessitates a different configuration for each. The rectilinear mass of three facades is broken on the fourth by a recessed courtyard containing the main entrance, marked by attached white marble columns. Even Orlov could not command the resources necessary for an interior comparable to the imperial palaces, yet the use of natural stone for the main stairway (in the style of the Italian Renaissance) and the elaborate stucco work remind of Orlov's imperial backing. Much of the palace was redecorated in 1844–1851 by Aleksandr Briullov, who preserved Rinaldi's design in a number of central spaces.

TRINITY CATHEDRAL, ALEXANDER NEVSKY MONASTERY. ST. PETERSBURG

Ivan Starov (1745–1808), graduated with distinction in 1762 from the Academy of Arts, where he studied with Kokorinov and Vallin de la Mothe. He subsequently spent four years in Paris in the studio of Charles de Wailly, and in 1766–68 traveled extensively in Italy. After his return to Petersburg, he accepted a teaching position at the Academy and in the early 1770s designed a number of country mansions in the environs of St. Petersburg and Moscow. His first major project in Petersburg was the Cathedral of the Trinity at the Alexander Nevsky Monastery, a project that had become enmeshed in a series of rejected proposals. Catherine, who approved Starov's project in 1776, was undoubtedly impressed by its monumental classicism, interpreted within a Roman basilical design. The great ribbed dome, on a rotunda with attached Corinthian columns over the main crossing, provides a contrast to the baroque dome of Rastrelli's Smolnyi cathedral, which soars above the center of a cross-inscribed structure. The greater amplitude and lower profile of the dome of the Trinity Cathedral suggests the work of Soufflot— particularly Ste. Geneviève (the Panthéon; 1755–1792)), whose design would likely have been seen by Starov during his stay in Paris.

Thus in retaining a basilical design Starov simply followed the original plan for the monastery developed by Trezzini. Yet no stylistic contrast could be greater— or more tactfully stated—than that between the early baroque designs by Trezzini, and Starov's neoclassical temple. For the west front, facing the spacious monastery yard, Starov created a hexastyle Tuscan Doric portico that frames the main

St. Petersburg   Trinity Cathedral, Alexander Nevsky Monastery. 1776–90

entrance and is itself framed by two square bell towers outlined with Corinthian pilasters. This harmonious balance of elements provides a clearly articulated surface on which Fedot Shubin, one of the leading Russian sculptors, created a series of panels with Biblical themes.

CHURCH OF JOHN THE BAPTIST AT CHESME PALACE.
ST. PETERSBURG

With the conclusion of the Russo-Turkish war in 1774 Georg Friedrich Veldten was commissioned to build a palace commemorating the Russian naval victory over the Turks at Chesme Bay in the Aegean (June 1770). The pseudo-Gothic style not only symbolized the exoticism of Turkish architecture but also reflected the Anglomania that significantly influenced the design of Catherine's palaces and the parks surrounding them. The Chesme Palace, completed in 1777, was intended not as a major imperial residence but as a transit palace to be used as a resting place during the annual shift of the court from Petersburg to the suburban palace at Tsarskoe Selo, and it was substantially altered in the 1830s for conversion into a veterans' hospital.

Much closer to its original form is the adjoining Church of John the Baptist, built between 1777 and 1780 in a style similar to that of Strawberry Hill Gothic. The finials, spires, and lancet windows are placed upon a structure whose quatrefoil design is reminiscent of certain private estate churches in the "Moscow baroque" style of the late seventeenth century. Indeed, it could be argued that the experi-

St. Petersburg   Church of John the Baptist at Chesme Palace. 1777–80. Southwest view.

mentation with unusual church forms during Catherine's reign reflects the increasing secularization of the upper nobility at the turn of the eighteenth century. Certainly the decorative panoply of the miniature Chesme church resembles the pseudo-Gothic pavilions that proliferated in estate parks during the reign of Catherine and thereafter.

PETROVSKY TRANSIT PALACE. MOSCOW

Matvei Kazakov was one of the most distinguished of Moscow's neoclassical architects, yet his first major work was in the pseudo-Gothic style. The Petrovsky Transit Palace, built in 1775–1782 on the northern outskirts of Moscow, was commissioned for Catherine's use during her visits to Moscow. Kazakov's palace combined the fashion for the Gothic revival with motifs drawn from medieval Russian architecture—such as the use of limestone ornament on brick walls and the flared columns on the main facade. Although the sharply-defined pitched gables and dormers project a fragmented appearance, the exterior is unified by a large dome over the rotunda at the center of the structure, with lavish plaster decoration. The Petrovsky Palace plan includes flanking, turreted wings that extend from the main facade to a low semicircular sweep with two guard towers at the entrance gates. Despite the "gothick" style associated with country estate architecture, the peculiar design of the palace owes much to the baroque—particularly in the window surrounds beneath the dome.

Moscow   Petrovsky Transit Palace. 1775–82

TSARITSYNO ESTATE. MOSCOW

The imperial estate of Tsaritsyno, situated to the south of central Moscow, was purchased in 1775 by Catherine the Great, who intended to create here a complex of palaces, pavilions, and service buildings rivaling the imperial estates near Petersburg. In this wooded setting, marked by ravines and a small river, she chose to dispense with the her neoclassical preferences in favor of the so-called Moorish-Gothic style. The architect Vasily Bazhenov's idiosyncratic design blends old Muscovite motifs with pseudo-gothic elements. His materials—unstuccoed brick and limestone—are in the tradition of Muscovite architecture of the sixteenth and seventeenth centuries.

Bazhenov's inventive imagination appears on a large scale in the kitchen and service wing (*Khlebnyi dom*), begun in 1784. Designed in the form of a quadrangle with rounded corners, the building contained two stories with lancet windows on the first floor and trefoil windows on the upper story. Although less inventive in its limestone detail than the smaller pavilions, the service wing was connected to the main palace compound by a colonnade and gate that comprise one of the most bizarre forms in Russian architecture: a semi-circular brick arch studded with limestone "teeth," flanked by intertwined coronets.

The final flurry of construction during 1784 (in preparation for a state visit by the Empress in 1785) gave rise to other structures whose elaborate limestone figures have suggested to some the cryptic symbols of Freemasonry, to which Bazhenov belonged. The most flamboyant is the "bridge over the ravine" with

Moscow   Bridge over the Ravine, Tsaritsyno.

Moscow   Imperial palace, Tsaritsyno estate. 1786–93

radiant bursts of limestone emanating from the arches on either end and an array of ornament resembling folk art. Hardly had the walls been completed for most of the structures, when Catherine, for reasons that remain unclear, halted construction after her inspection visit of 1785. She commanded that the centerpiece of the ensemble—the imperial palaces—be razed, and in 1786 entrusted their rebuilding to Matvei Kazakov, Bazhenov's assistant.

Kazakov in his turn conceived a monumental, if less imaginative, palace that combined the Gothic with obvious elements of the classical order system, particularly in the columns of the projecting square towers (figure 34). Kazakov already had one major pseudo-gothic work to his credit—the Petrovsky Transit Palace (1775–1782). Thus the new design was readily produced, and work began on the then leveled site in 1786. However, the outbreak of the Second Russo-Turkish War in 1791 again led to reduced means and further delays. The walls of the two-story palace were covered with a temporary roof in 1793; and after Catherine's death in 1796, the project was canceled, thus leaving a grand and bizarre set of ruins that continue to amaze visitors.

CAMERON GALLERY. TSARSKOE SELO

Charles Cameron (1743–1812), an enigmatic Scotsman brought to Russia by Catherine the Great, had spent several years in Rome, where he studied the classical monuments as well as the work of Palladio. Cameron arrived in Petersburg apparently in 1779 and worked in Russia over the next two decades. Among his greatest monuments is the Cameron Gallery, connected to the Catherine Palace at Tsarskoe Selo. In a brilliant statement of contrasts, Cameron designed a ground floor of massive rusticated Pudost stone, surmounted by a delicate peristyle of 44 Ionic columns. As an addition to the original design, Cameron made use of the slope of the land toward the Great Pond to create in 1786 a monumental entrance on the east facade: one flight of steps leading to the ground level, and two in an oval sweep leading to the upper floor. The dominant architectural elements of the magnificent east facade—the arched entry on the ground level and the portico with four Ionic columns—are repeated on the long side facades (north and south) in the form of a ground arcade and two slightly projected tetrastyle porticos on the upper level. The width of the upper floor is divided into three equilateral bays, the middle of which is enclosed with large French windows providing an unobstructed view of the natural park that had been created around the Great Pond in the 1770s.

The exterior gallery served for the contemplation not only of nature but also of the classical civilization. The collection of more than 50 bronze busts of ancient philosophers, poets, and rulers placed along the colonnade provides a guide to the assimilation of classical culture during the reign of Catherine, an ideological background for the development of neoclassical architecture in Russia. After the completion of the gallery in 1787, a final antique touch was provided by the addition at the southwest corner of a rusticated *pente douce* (1792–1794), whose gradual incline allowed the aged empress easier access to the park.

Tsarskoe Selo   Cameron Gallery. 1780–86

PAVLOVSK PALACE

Perhaps the greatest single monument of Palladianism in Russia is the palace that Charles Cameron built at Pavlovsk, to the south of St. Petersburg, for Grand Duke Paul. Although the palace, built in 1782–1786, was not completed to the original specifications, and although Cameron was frequently at odds with Paul and Maria Fedorovna—who had far fewer resources than did Catherine—the central structure provides fair measure of Cameron's adaptation of the Palladian ideal. A two-storied portico composed of paired Corinthian columns dominates the courtyard facade, which was originally flanked by one-story galleries leading to service wings on either side. The more impressive view, however, is of the opposite facade—again a Corinthian portico, of paired and single columns supporting a pediment. From this perspective ornamental trees obscure later additions by Vincenzo Brenna (see below) and allow a clearer perception of Cameron's building, surmounted with a rotunda and colonnade. By virtue of its detail as well as its site, a knoll descending to the Slavianka River, the palace suggests Palladio's design for the Villa Trissino at Meledo.

The interior of the main palace was designed in a general sense by Cameron; but because of the increasingly difficult relations between the architect and the grand duke and duchess, Cameron succeeded in completing only a few major rooms in the imperial suite on the ground floor overlooking the park: the White Dining

Pavlovsk   Imperial palace. 1782–86

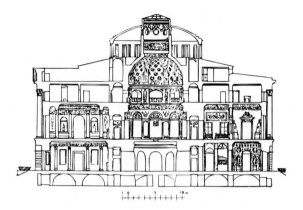

Pavlovsk   Imperial palace. Plan.

Room, the Billiard Room, the Old Drawing Room, and the Ballroom. Each of these rooms was designed with consummate taste and skill, but without the bold inventiveness of Cameron's rooms at Tsarskoe Selo. In addition Cameron provided the design for the Egyptian Vestibule—the main entrance to the palace from the courtyard—with replicas of ancient Egyptian statues by Ivan Prokofiev and plaster medallions of the signs of the zodiac. Of particular note is Carlo Scotti's ceiling painting, in grisaille, of the Four Seasons with a trompe l'oeil architectural figure in the center. By 1787, however, the preference of Paul and Maria Fedorovna for the work of Cameron's assistant, Vincenzo Brenna, led to the latter's increasing role in the design of the interior, and in 1789 Brenna had become the de facto architect in charge of palace construction at Pavlovsk.

PASHKOV HOUSE. MOSCOW

Among the last major monuments in Moscow to be attributed to Bazhenov, the Pashkov House (1784–1788) marks a reaffirmation of neoclassicism. Built as Bazhenov's work at Tsaritsyno reached its culmination, the stuccoed brick mansion for Life Guards Captain P. E. Pashkov represents Moscow's answer to the palaces of Petersburg. Even the style of the Pashkov mansion is distinct from Petersburg architecture and reminds of the English baroque at the turn of the eighteenth century. The two wings, with Ionic porticoes, are separated from the main structure by rusticated galleries, whose length is half that of the central facade. This distance, and its relation to the height of the wings, creates a balanced system of proportions uniting the three elements. While each of the component parts has sufficient space to be appreciated separately, one is always aware of their relation to the whole.

I. I. BARYSHNIKOV HOUSE. MOSCOW

The spacious territory for the house for Matvei Kazakov's merchant patron Ivan Baryshnikov on Miasnitsky Street, to the northeast of central Moscow, permitted the creation of a front courtyard, framed by entrance gates and pylons, with flank-

Moscow   Pashkov Mansion. 1784–88

Moscow   I. I. Baryshnikov mansion. 1793–1802

ing two-storied wings. As was common in Moscow, the mansion grew in stages, between 1793 and 1802, with the reconstruction and expansion of earlier structures on the site. Consequently traces of different stylistic tendencies are evident, culminating in the project's central, unifying element: the elevated portico of Corinthian columns in the major order. Designed in Kazakov's best Palladian manner, with columns paired at either end, the projecting portico and frieze represent a late development in eighteenth-century Moscow neoclassicism—as does the mezzanine above the main floor (all of these elements were among the last phase of rebuilding). As in Kazakov's other mansions, the strong pediment replaces the dome of the rotunda that defined the central mass of his major public buildings; yet circular and oval forms figured largely in the design of the interior, particularly the great main hall, or ballroom.

OSTANKINO PALACE. MOSCOW

Having formed at Kuskovo the leading serf theatrical troupe in Russia, Nikolai Sheremetev in 1792 undertook the construction of a palace-theater at his neighboring estate of Ostankino, a former Cherkassky village whose Church of the Trinity exemplifies the late seventeenth-century ornamental style. Sheremetev, the owner of 210,000 serfs and vast land holdings, could well afford to build an entire estate around a theater, and the dimensions of the central structure, culminating in a rotunda, are much larger than those of the Kuskovo mansion. Several architects submitted proposals, including Giacomo Quarenghi, author of a number of major projects in Moscow. The basic plan for the structure, its facades, and the adjoining park is attributed to Francesco Camporesi, although during the course of its implementation over the next six years, Sheremetev turned to Quarenghi, Karl Blank,

Moscow   Ostankino Palace. 1792–1800

Moscow   Ostankino Palace. Interior, theater.

and even Vincenzo Brenna for modifications, as well as additions to the wings. The actual construction was supervised by Sheremetev's serf architects Aleksei Mironov, Grigory Dikushin, and, above all, Pavel Argunov (son of the painter Ivan Argunov), who had apprenticed with Vasily Bazhenov in Petersburg.

The entire ensemble of palace and pavilions at Ostankino was created within the space of a decade. The central building is marked by an elevated portico of six Corinthian columns and culminates in a rotunda with Palladian overtones (for all of its monumental appearance, with structure is built of wood covered with stucco). This establishes an imposing center for a series of wings and attached pavilions that were used for living space. The interior is dominated by the theater, which is two stories in height and extends across much of the central block. The floor of the theater (whose main axis is perpendicular to that of the portico) was ingeniously designed to serve also as grand ballroom. The upper floor consists of an enfilade of state rooms that open onto the portico, and a picture gallery.

On the ground floor, galleries extend from either side of the central structure to the two main pavilions: the Italian (west), with a sculpture gallery; and the Egyptian (east), containing a concert hall. The west facade of the Italian Pavilion ends in a rotunda, and the large windows of both pavilions are particularly effective in achieving a union between the luxuriant interior and the park beyond. Indeed, the main rectangle of the park, enclosed on three sides by trees and lined with statuary, has been characterized as a "quasi-interior" space. The harmony of park and palace is facilitated by the unity of the park facade, defined by a grand loggia of ten Ionic columns and a mammoth pediment with the carved coat of arms. Projecting wings with porticoes frame the facade and visually separate the structure from the attached wings and pavilions.

The facades of the palace and its pavilions are liberally decorated with statuary placed in niches, as well as friezes depicting classical tableaux, such as the bas reliefs of sacrifice to Jupiter and Demeter by Fedor Gordeev and Gavrill Zamaraev. In 1801 Alexander I visited Ostankino as a part of his coronation ceremonies; but soon after this august occasion, the theater waned after the illness and death in 1803 of Zhemchugova, the leading actress of the troupe and Nikolai Sheremetev's wife. After Sheremetev's own premature death in 1809, the palace remained in the family as little more than a unused monument to the brilliance of a culture fostered by the Russian nobility at its zenith.

ZOLOTAREV HOUSE. KALUGA

Although a provincial town to the south of Moscow, Kaluga in the eighteenth century had a considerable wealth that was reflected in mansions, commissioned primarily by merchants, whose scale and style imitated grand residences in Moscow. The most impressive among them is the Zolotarev house, built in 1805–1808 by an unknown architect for the merchant P. M. Zolotarev, son of a noted Kaluga silversmith. The two-storied stuccoed brick structure is situated flush with the street line and flanked by two arched entryways that lead to a courtyard and park extending to the banks of the Oka River. The center of this villa is marked by a pediment and slightly recessed pilasters that create three segments, each of which

Kaluga   Zolotarev house. 1805–1808

contains a high-relief plaster panel on themes from the *Iliad*: the quarrel of the god-desses, the judgement of Paris, and the Sacrifice. The flanking entryways, with wrought-iron tracery, are decorated with trumpeting figures, and the entrances to the house on the side facades, are framed by cast iron porte-cocheres. The interior was decorated by the Moscow firm of S. P. Campioni and contained furnishings in the Empire style.

CATHEDRAL OF SAINTS BORIS AND GLEB. TORZHOK

Although little known outside of Russia, Nikolai Lvov was one of the greatest of neoclassical architects produced in the reign of Catherine the Great. Like his dis-tinguished contemporaries, he worked in St. Petersburg; but his best work was done in the country, particularly in Tver Province (between Moscow and St. Petersburg), whose concentration of wealthy estates is reflected in the richness of such monuments as the Cathedral of Sts. Boris and Gleb (1785–96) at the monastery of the same name in Torzhok. In a display of the neoclassical aesthetic at its purest, the hexastyle Tuscan portico on the west facade of the cathedral is repeated on the east (apsidal) facade. The porticoes provide a transition to the cen-tral dome, which rests above a polygonal drum with a large thermal window. For all of its neoclassical rigor, the cathedral also reflects elements of Russo-Byzantine architecture, not only in the centralized plan, but also the appearance on the exte-rior corners of arched bays reminiscent of the cathedrals of twelfth-century Novgorod.

Torzhok   Cathedral of Sts. Boris and Gleb. 1785–96. Northwest view.

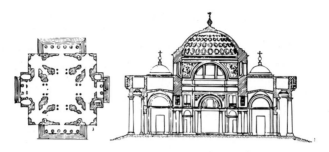

Torzhok   Cathedral of Sts. Boris and Gleb. Section, plan.

Within the Torzhok cathedral the massive split-corner piers are faced with Doric columns that support open arches over the arms of the cross. The arches in turn lead upward to the thermal windows and the central coffered dome, which on the interior is hemispherical. The classical rigor of the design is clearly stated and refers both to the Pantheon and the thermae, yet the interior space is as appropriate to the needs of the Orthodox liturgy as was the Hagia Sophia and other Byzantine models that laid the basis for Russian church architecture.

CATHEDRAL OF THE KAZAN MOTHER OF GOD. ST. PETERSBURG

Commissioned in 1800, the Kazan Cathedral is the most imposing of Petersburg's neoclassical churches. As early as the 1780s there had been plans to rebuild Mikhail Zemtsov's modest Church of the Nativity of the Virgin on Nevsky Prospekt, the repository of the Icon of the Kazan Mother of God, which had been brought to the city by Peter the Great and was considered the palladium of the Romanovs. In 1799 Emperor Paul reopened the competition for a cathedral whose design would reflect his desire for a reconciliation with Roman Catholicism and,

St. Petersburg   Cathedral of the Kazan Mother of God. 1801–11. North view.

implicitly, to establish his capital as a new Rome. After a complicated process, a committee headed by Count Alexander Stroganov chose Andrei Voronikhin, a brilliantly gifted former serf of the Stroganov family.

Voronikhin's design embodies monumental classicism as interpreted in Saint Peter's in Rome and Jacques Germain Soufflot's Sainte Geneviève in Paris (1755–1792). Conceptually, Voronikhin's sole predecessor in a Roman classical exercise of this magnitude was Bazhenov, whose designs may well have influenced Voronikhin. The body of the Kazan Cathedral is in the form of a Latin cross, with Corinthian porticoes on the north, south, and west, and a semicircular apse, with attic frieze, on the east. The structure is surmounted by a large attic. Over the crossing is an elongated, narrow dome above a drum whose pilasters echo the rows of columns below.

Voronikhin's ingenuity was taxed by the problem of adapting the cathedral to its setting. Although Nevsky Prospekt was marked by a number of palaces, the street was not particularly imposing at the beginning of the nineteenth century; the Kazan Cathedral was to be the first of its great monuments. Because the cathedral's main axis—east-west as dictated by Orthodox tradition—parallels the Prospekt, the architect had to create a more striking resolution for the cathedral's north facade, facing the street, than for its actual main entrance on the west. His

St. Petersburg   Cathedral of the Kazan Mother of God. Interior.

solution is a vast curving colonnade, anchored at the east and west ends by a portico of square pylons, culminating in an attic frieze. With its sharply defined entablature and balustrade, the Corinthian colonnade sweeps from both ends toward the north portico and dome, which are barely strong enough to focus the energy released along this grand arc. In the original plan there was to be a second colonnade on the south side, but because of cost overruns it remained unbuilt.

The brick walls of the structure are surfaced with Pudost stone, a limestone tufa obtained near Gatchina that is tractable when quarried but hardens on exposure to air, thus providing an ideal substance for detailed sculpting. Voronikhin exploited these properties in designing friezes on Biblical subjects for the east and west end blocks and the apse, as well as sculpted panels for the three porticoes. The exterior columns and capitals, arranged in ranks of four, are also of Pudost stone, and various details are rendered in granite (three different types), limestone, and marble. Bronze was extensively used for statuary, including statues of the "national" saints Vladimir and Alexander Nevsky, placed on either side of the north portal. The massive doors of the north portal were covered with bronze panels, which Voronikhin based on Lorenzo Ghiberti's designs for the doors of the Baptistery in Florence.

The interior is centered around the cupolar space, defined by massive pylons, above which the pendentives with Evangelists support a drum with a grisaille frieze of scenes from the life of Christ. The Cathedral of the Kazan Mother of God was intended as a monument specifically to the divine protection extended to the Romanov dynasty, and it would appear that no cost was spared to endow the interior with a magnificent and palatial finish, even to gilding the bronze capitals of the interior colonnade. From the coffered, double-shelled cupola to the 56 paired Corinthian columns of polished red granite, 10.7 meters in height, that line the central nave and arms of the cruciform structure, the massive luxuriance of the cathedral proclaims the immutable power of state and religion. Even the massive barrel vaults seem weightless with their network of hexagonal coffering and inset rosettes. The painting of the interior, supervised by the Academy of Arts, included works on canvas as well as on plaster.

THE EXCHANGE (BOURSE). ST. PETERSBURG

Thomas de Thomon's Bourse displays a familiarity with the temples at Paestum, which exerted a major influence of the development of European neoclassicism as a noble "archaic" style at the end of the eighteenth century. The massive base of red granite supports a peristyle of 44 Tuscan Doric columns. The peristyle encloses rusticated stuccoed brick walls, at each end of which, above the entablature, stands allegorical statuary representing maritime commerce. In its apparent simplicity, the Bourse is admirably conceived to anchor the tip of Petersburg's largest island, the central element in the expanse of water between the Peter-Paul Fortress and the imperial monuments on the left bank of the Neva. To emphasize this strategic point, Thomon placed two rostral columns on either side of the Bourse, with allegorical figures at their base personifying Russia's major rivers. In addition to their monumental decorative function the columns, which have spiral staircases on the interior) were to serve as beacons, and during national holidays they are still lit.

St. Petersburg   The Exchange. 1805–10

On the interior the Stock Exchange was designed with a spacious trading hall, whose ceiling consisted of a single coffered barrel vault. Each end of the main hall leads into a vestibule of the same width and also barrel-vaulted, but on an axis perpendicular to the central space. Three stories of offices extend the length of the building on either side of the central halls. Natural light for the interior is admitted by a rectangular skylight and by large semicircular fan windows on either end, whose form is repeated on the inner wall between the vestibule and main hall. Within this precise rectangular structure the semicircle is a recurrent motif, in the fan windows that extend along the upper walls of the side facades as well as in the relieving arches above the keystone pediments of the large first-floor windows. Thus every element of the exterior is calculated with attention to geometric proportions as well as to the creative tension between the contrasting vectors of curve and straight line.

THE ADMIRALTY. ST. PETERSBURG

From the beginnings of St. Petersburg, the docks and administrative building known as the Admiralty had been an essential part of the city's existence. They were first built by Peter the Great and then rebuilt, in the 1730s, by Ivan Korobov. By 1806 plans submitted by Andreian Zakharov for a reconstruction of the large, decrepit complex had been approved. Zakharov attended the Academy of Arts in St. Petersburg, and studied extensively in France and Italy. Although he died in 1811, long before the completion of the building in 1823, no significant changes were made in his design.

St. Petersburg   The Admiralty. 1810–23

In reconstructing Korobov's partially destroyed Admiralty, Zakharov expanded the length of the facade from 300 meters to 375—a quarter of a mile. In addition there were two perpendicular wings almost half that long extending to the river. From the perspective of the Neva River, the complex consisted of two pi-shaped buildings, one within the other, which were originally separated by a narrow canal. The inner building served the Admiralty dockyard, which it enclosed on three sides, while the outer contained administrative offices. On the other side was a large square—now a park—on which fronts the main facade. Its center is marked by a tower and spire, which envelop Korobov's original tower, and contains an arch, flanked by statues of nymphs supporting the globe (sculptor: Feodosy Shchedrin). The attic frieze portrays Neptune handing Peter the Great the trident, symbol of power over the seas. Above the corners of the attic are statues of Alexander the Great, Ajax, Achilles, and Pyrrhus. The base of the spire rests on an Ionic peristyle, whose cornice supports twenty-eight allegorical and mythological statues representing the seasons, the elements, the winds.

On either side of the tower a rusticated ground floor defines the base of the main facade, above which are two rows of simply articulated windows. (Later a third row of windows replaced the stucco frieze that had originally run along the upper part of the facade.) At each end of the facade is a self-contained unit, marked by a dodecastyle Doric portico with a pediment containing a sculpted frieze. Each of the perpendicular wings has a similar Doric portico of twelve columns, and each culminates at the Neva in an end block, with a rusticated arch flanked by Doric columns.

The Admiralty end blocks are one of the most radical attempts to achieve a monumental purity of volume idealized at the end of the eighteenth century. And therein lies the key to the remarkable power of the Admiralty building: Zakharov

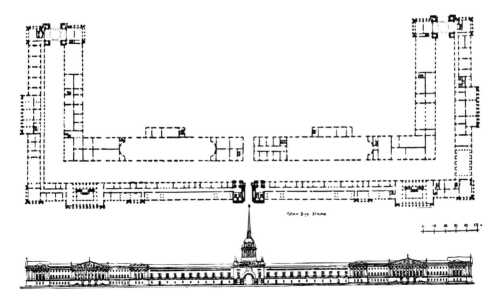

St. Petersburg Admiralty.

St. Petersburg   The Admiralty. 1810–23

had solved the problem of horizontal repetition by applying classical orders to simple geometric forms, and yet the simplicity of the surfaces provided the ideal setting for Zakharov's large rusticated arches and high-relief sculpture. The use of portico, pavilion, and spire, the restrained window detail, the placing of heroic sculpture on pediments and at the base of the spire produce both visual stimulation and a sense of absolute control.

THE BUILDING OF THE GENERAL STAFF. ST. PETERSBURG

Carlo Rossi received his early architectural training from Vincenzo Brenna at Pavlovsk and other imperial projects. In 1802 Brenna and Rossi left for a three-year sojourn in Europe (Florence, Rome, Paris). After 1814, he rapidly assumed a position of authority in the implementation of Alexander's general plan for St. Petersburg. Concurrently with the construction of the Mikhailovsky Palace (now the Russian Museum), Rossi undertook a far greater project. The area between the south facade of the Winter Palace and the Moika Canal had been partially developed, but no comprehensive plan for the space had yet been implemented. Rossi's task—which began in 1819 and was completed in 1829—consisted of two parts: to construct an administrative complex for the for the General Staff and the Ministries of Finance and Foreign affairs; and, in so doing, to create an appropri-

St. Petersburg The Building of the General Staff.

ately imposing public square in front of the Winter Palace. His solution called for the ministerial complex, subsequently known as the Building of the Main Staff, to take the form of a large arc facing the palace. The interior configuration of the complex consists of a system of courtyards and light wells formed by perpendicular extensions that link the main facade with adjacent structures on the Moika Canal and Nevsky Prospekt.

The center of the main facade is dominated by a triumphal arch, surmounted by a chariot of victory. In the design of the arch Rossi not only centered the enormous facade but linked it to the surrounding area, particularly by the passageway through the triumphal arch, leading from Palace Square to Nevsky Prospekt. The passageway is composed of a series of three arches, the first two of which are located on an axis with the central gates to the Winter Palace, while the last follows the turn of the passage toward the Prospekt. The light that enters the spaces between the arches enhances the perception of depth and illuminates the decorative detail of this unique procession of framed space toward the city's main square.

The Palace Square facade of the General Staff building—devoid of decoration except for a cornice frieze, a balustrade, and columns flanking the arch—forms the ideal complement to the baroque panoply of Rastrelli's Winter Palace. The color scheme for this and for most of Rossi's other monuments was to be light gray with white trim, but later generations have preferred more assertive tones: yellow with white trim, and the metallic sculpture of military regalia painted black. Yet more important than the color is the contour of the main facade, which not only imposes order over a vast urban space but also channels movement toward Nevsky Prospekt, the main thoroughfare of the city.

IMPERIAL COURT STABLES. ST. PETERSBURG

During the last great phase of neoclassical architecture in St. Petersburg, the work of Carlo Rossi was complemented by that of Vasily Stasov, who was particularly adept in applying monumental classical forms to prosaic structures such as markets and warehouses. In 1817–1823 he rebuilt the Imperial Court Stables, originally built in 1720–1723 by Nicholas Friedrich Göbel on the Moika Canal, near the Winter Palace. Stasov preserved the foundation and much of the walls of the complex plan. The Doric loggias of the end blocks support recessed thermal windows that rise above the cornice binding most of the structure. Every detail of the exterior clarifies and enriches the form of the building, whose central point is the large cuboid Church of the Miraculous Icon of the Savior, with a low dome and Ionic loggia. The iconography of the stucco panels (by Demut-Malinovsky) on either side of the loggia is evocative of burden of carrying: on the right the Entry of Christ into Jerusalem and on the left the Christ Bearing the Cross.

CATHEDRAL OF THE TRINITY. ST PETERSBURG

Among Vasily Stasov's numerous churches, the largest is the Cathedral of the Trinity (1828–1835), which is to this day one of the most prominent landmarks of the southern part of the old city. Supported by an elite regiment, the Izmailovsky,

St. Petersburg   Imperial Court Stables, Church of the Icon of the Savior. 1817–23. South view.

the church was originally built in wood with an unusual (for a Russian church) cruciform plan. Stasov reproduced the plan with mighty hexastyle Corinthian porticos extending the width of each arm of the cross. The upper walls of the entire structure are banded by a stucco frieze with festoons comparable to those of Rossi's Alexandrine theater; but the white walls are otherwise as clear as those of early medieval churches, with only a single large arched window on each surface.

St. Petersburg   Cathedral of the Trinity. 1828–35

The dark blue metal domes are arranged at the points of the compass, as dictated by the plan of the church.

The most impressive feature of the Izmailovsky Trinity Cathedral is the central dome (over 26 meters in diameter), whose size and detail resemble those of Starov's Trinity Cathedral and the Kazan Cathedral; yet no other pentacupolar church in Petersburg achieves the same pyramidal effect through the spacing and size of the subsidiary domes in relation to the main. The colonnade of Corinthian columns attached to the drum beneath the dome conveys the sense of a large rotunda, clearly seen by virtue of its high elevation above the central crossing and the relatively small size of the flanking cupolas. On the interior the cruciform design is accented by paired columns at the main points of the plan.

BOLSHOI THEATER. MOSCOW

After the fire of 1812 in Moscow, government authorities and planners modified aspects of the city's central area without fundamentally changing its concentric ring pattern. The reconstruction effort often involved the creation of new structures, but in exceptional cases damaged landmarks were rebuilt in the same style. Among those who participated in this herculean task, none was more influential than Osip Bove, who supervised the formation of one of Moscow's great public spaces, Theater Square, intended as an appropriate setting for the revived Petrovsky Theater (subsequently known as the Bolshoi), which had burned in 1805 and not been rebuilt. The new theater (1821–1824) was designed by the Petersburg architect Andrei Mikhailov and by Bove, with a grand Ionic portico surmounted by a statue of Apollo in a quadriga.

This late neoclassical form has not survived in its original state: a fire in 1853 destroyed the entire interior of the theater, and when rebuilt by Albert Kavos in the 1850s, the main facade was substantially modified by the addition of Renaissance elements characteristic of the succeeding era of eclecticism. The buildings flanking Theater Square were planned as uniform, subordinate structures, two-storied with a ground floor arcade. The plan was never entirely realized, and the neoclassical architecture has since been much modified, with the partial exception of the building now housing the Malyi (small) Theater.

Moscow   Bolshoi Theater. 1821–24; 1850s

MOSCOW UNIVERSITY.

Another example of the re-creation of a monument destroyed in 1812 is the main building of Moscow University, originally designed by Matvei Kazakov and rebuilt in 1817–1819 by Domenico Gilardi. Gilardi wisely followed the general configuration of Kazakov's monumental structure, yet introduced significant changes that made the design his own. The central portico, elevated on a limestone base, was enlarged and its columns were re-erected in the Greek Doric order (Kazakov had used Ionic) with bold channeling. Behind the columns, the richly-figured frieze, portraying the nine muses, was designed by the sculptor Gavriil Zamaraev, who had worked with Kazakov on the interior decoration of the main hall of the Kremlin Senate. As if to accentuate the plasticity of the portico, Gilardi eliminated most of the decoration (such as Kazakov's pilasters) from the remainder of the facade, with the exception of masks on the keystones above the windows of the rusticated first floor and other minor ornamentation between the upper windows.

Behind the portico of the university building Gilardi increased the size of the dome over the main Ceremonial Hall. This allowed a greater pitch of the interior dome (in fact a half dome), for which he designed Moscow's crowning master-piece of trompe l'oeil painting in a monumental sculpted style. The curved space is delineated by ribs, within which is an elaborate pattern of rhomboids with inset

Moscow University   1817–19

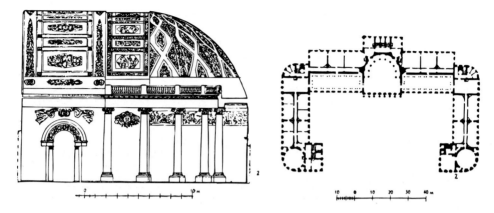

Moscow University   Plan and rotunda section.

figures—all in grisaille. Friezes at the base of the dome, also in grisaille, allegorically depict the arts and sciences, as well as classical philosophers and Apollo with the muses.

A. P. KHRUSHCHEV HOUSE. MOSCOW

After the 1812 fire, fashionable residential areas underwent a major reconstruction, with new houses often arising on the foundations of those gutted by the fire. Some of the best extant examples have been attributed to Afanasy Grigorev, such

Moscow University   Ceremonial Hall.

Moscow   A. P. Khrushchev house. 1814–15

as the house built in 1814–1815 for retired Guards officer A. P. Khrushchev. Constructed of logs, with the upper walls stuccoed and detailed to resemble masonry, the one-story house with mezzanine was built on the vaulted limestone basement level of the pre-war structure. Its corner location on Prechistenka Street offered the opportunity, exploited by Grigorev, of creating two "main" facades, each with an Ionic portico. Neither in fact frames the entrance, which is situated to the side of the house facing Khrushchev Lane. This facade might therefore be assigned priority, as indicated by its four pairs of Ionic columns beneath a sculpted pediment and by the curved terrace that serves as a base for the facade as well as a transition to Prechistenka Street. The second portico, facing Prechistenka, functions as a support for the mezzanine balcony, thus allowing the inhabitants an elevated view of the busy street below.

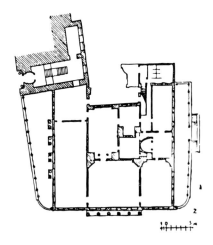

Moscow   A. P. Khrushchev house. Plan.

The plan of the Khrushchev house contains a compact enfilade of rooms facing Prechistenka, and, at a right angle, a ballroom extending for most of the front of the house. The state rooms display much the same approach to design found in the larger mansions: ceilings with painted arabesques and trompe l'oeil motifs, inset columns supporting architraves, and elaborate plaster molding. The form of this house is typical of other residences of the period, in which comfort and financial constraints began to determine new forms of spatial arrangements.

PROVISION WAREHOUSES. MOSCOW

Before 1812 Vasily Stasov divided his time between Moscow, Petersburg, and Europe (primarily Italy); but after the loss of his home in the 1812 fire, Stasov moved to St. Petersburg and made a brilliant architectural career. Among his contributions to the reconstruction of Moscow, his greatest achievement comes from a series of designs (1816–21) for provision warehouses, originally intended for Petersburg. When the need arose to build space for army provisions storage in Moscow at the end of the 1820s, Stasov's final warehouse variant of 1821 served as a basis.

The actual construction of the Provision Warehouses in 1829–1831 was implemented by Fedor Shestakov; but the design bears the stamp of Stasov's genius, which combined the functional requirements of the warehouse with the archaic clarity of the Doric order, imposed on a structural mass with little ornament. The Moscow warehouse consists of three large two-story buildings with tapered walls and main portals in a manner considered "Egyptian." The portals are surmounted by pediments and a recessed window arch, but there are no columns; only the entablature specifies the Doric order. The hipped roofs, with ventilation dormers, serve to accent both the mass of the ensemble and the proportional relations among the three components. The Provision Warehouses achieve a combination of the aesthetic and the useful that was considered a guiding ideal of classical architecture.

NEOCLASSICAL ARCHITECTURE IN KOSTROMA

Perhaps the most coherent of the neoclassical plans designed for provincial cities in the late 18th century was that of Kostroma, located at the confluence of the Kostroma and Volga Rivers. The plan, developed in 1781–1784, left intact the

Moscow   Provision Warehouses. 1821; 1829–31

Kostroma   Red Arcade bell tower. 1792. Trifle Trading Rows. 1820s

Kostroma   Fire Tower. 1823–26

medieval kremlin and its Dormition Cathedral, but established immediately to the north a new center, from which radiated twelve streets. Over the next five decades, a number of architects reconstructed the town center according to the plan.

The central square of Kostroma was bordered by a series of trading rows, which were typically named after their primary commodity: the Flour (Large and Small), Fish, Gingerbread, Butter, and Vegetable, or Tobacco (to a plan by the Petersburg architect Vasily Stasov), in addition to the Trifle and the Red arcades. The visual dominant of the west side of the Red arcade is a bell tower, constructed in 1792 by S. Vorotilov adjacent to the small pentacupolar Church of the Transfiguration on the Rows, dating from the early part of the century. The result demonstrates a sensitivity to the scale and complementary form of earlier Russian architectural forms.

Perhaps the most distinctive work of Kostroma neoclassicism is the main fire station and tower, built in 1823–1826 by P. I. Fursov. The main building, for administrative offices and housing for the firefighters, resembles a classical temple, with an Ionic portico. Above the pediment is a low rusticated block that serves as a base for the watch tower, with a rusticated shaft and volutes supporting the observation platform. On either side of the central block, one-story arcaded stables and a carriage shed extend symmetrically.

10. NINETEENTH CENTURY: ECLECTICISM

GREAT KREMLIN PALACE. MOSCOW

Concurrently with work on the Church of Christ the Savior, Nicholas initiated the rebuilding of the Great Kremlin Palace, which had been severely damaged in the 1812 occupation and subsequently repaired. In 1838 Konstantin Ton assumed the project, which provided a imposing facade for the Kremlin above the Moscow River, and created a stylistic link with the Terem Palace, the Faceted Chambers, and the Annunciation Cathedral within the interior of the Kremlin. The stylization was most closely related to the ornate but uniform window surrounds of the seventeenth-century Terem Palace, which Ton repeated on a much larger scale. For the design of the interior of the Great Kremlin Palace, Ton was joined by the court architect Friedrich Richter, who combined neoclassical, baroque, gothic, and medieval Russian motifs. As an "archaic," historical device Ton freely used elaborate barrel and groin vaults for the main halls, of which the grandest is the two-storied Hall of St. George, in honor of recipients of the highest Russian military honor.

CATHEDRAL OF ST. ISAAC OF DALMATIA. ST. PETERSBURG

St. Isaac's Cathedral, the largest of Petersburg's churches, was rebuilt at least twice before Alexander I commissioned yet another, greatly expanded, version. In 1818 the project was awarded to the young French architect Auguste Ricard de Montferrand. The culmination of the structure was a large rotunda and dome flanked by four domes. As the plan was modified over the ensuing decade, the corner towers became much smaller and were relegated to use as bell cotes. The gilded ribbed dome, resting above a rotunda with monolithic Corinthian columns of red granite, was at the time of its construction one of the largest in Europe (almost 25.8 meters in outer diameter and 2226 metric tons in weight) and technically the most advanced in its triple-shelled iron form and truss system.

The west pediment contains the sculpted group "St. Isaac blessing the Emperor Theodosius and his wife Flaccilla," with its message of the union of sacred and

Moscow   Great Kremlin Palace. 1838–50s

St. Petersburg   Cathedral of St. Isaac of Dalmatia. 1818–58. South view.

St. Petersburg Cathedral of St. Isaac of Dalmatia. Interior.

secular. The exterior bronze sculpture—most of which was entrusted to Ivan Vitali—included statues for niches set within the marble-clad facades; figures of the apostles above the pediments, with the four Evangelists situated at the peak of each pediment; and angels at the corners and above the rotundal balustrade. Sculpted reliefs provide a narrative focus and weight to the pediments, which rest on monolithic red granite columns quarried near in Finland and each weighing some 114 metric tons.

The interior of the St. Isaac's Cathedral contains a bewildering array of precious metals and semi-precious stones (lapis lazuli, porphyry, marble, malachite) used to encrust the massive piers, the iconostasis, and the vaulting. The Russian love of color and narrative on church interiors, denied by the austerity of neoclassicism, here returns with a force amplified by technical means unknown to the medieval church. The malachite surfaces of the iconostasis columns and the pervasive use of gilt for architectural details are two of the more obvious examples. Among the paintings, which vary in quality, Karl Briullov's depiction of the Mother of God surrounded by a host of saints on the hemispherical inner dome remains the center of attention. The interior of St. Isaac's was also decorated with mosaic panels by Russian masters who mastered the technique after four years of study in the mid-1840s at the Barberi studio in Rome.

The completion of the Cathedral of St. Isaac established a new visual dominant in the Petersburg cityscape: its dome was visible from points throughout the city and its great mass defined both the south side of Senate Square but also the north side of the new St. Isaac's Square.

COURT STABLES. PETERHOF

In August 1847 Nicholas Benois was commissioned to build a new complex for the court stables at Peterhof. Proceeding from the tsar's fondness for the Gothic revival, Benois created one of the most imposing monuments sponsored by the imperial court at the middle of the century. The centerpiece of the Court Stables is the Manége, whose facade faces north, toward the Gulf of Finland. On the exterior the building (for riding demonstrations) displays lancet windows, pinnacles, and other typical decorative devices of the gothic revival, yet much of the facade is formed of durable cast iron—innovative for the time, although rust-stained now for lack of proper maintenance. In addition the sculptor David Jensen worked closely with Benois in fashioning the elaborate terra cotta details for the gothic window tracery of this, and other, structures of the ensemble. For the interior Benois designed an impressive timber hammerbeam roof.

The manege is flanked by living quarters which extend into two large court-yards containing the stables, carriage storage, workshops, and other service build-ings. Each of the courtyards is dominated by large square crenelated towers placed along a single east-west axis, and their lancet arches form a dramatic reced-ing perspective from one end of the ensemble to the other. The structures are of brick, with terra cotta, stucco, and iron detailing. Despite the apparent anomaly of using such an imposing complex for the shelter of horses and those who made their living from them, this historical reminiscence in architectural form suited his pretensions as a chivalric ruler.

Peterhof Court Stables.

MARIINSKY AND NEW MIKHAILOVSKY PALACES. ST. PETERSBURG

The most prominent designer of palaces in St. Petersburg in the mid-nineteenth century was Andrei Shtakenshneider. His first project for the imperial court was the Mariinsky Palace (1839–1844) built for the grand duchess Maria Nikolaevich on St. Isaac's Square opposite the cathedral. The design relies heavily on classical elements such as Corinthian columns and pilasters; yet there are fundamental differences with neoclassicism. Although the center of the building is clearly defined, it lacks the emphasis that neoclassical architects created by means of a pediment

St. Petersburg Mariinsky Palace. 1839–44

St. Petersburg   New Mikhailovsky Palace. 1857–61

and by highlighting elements in white on a pastel background. For the facade
Shtakenshneider used a local reddish-brown sandstone, considered easier to
maintain than stucco over brick. Other Renaissance motifs appear in the ornamental details, and the general design derives from the seventeenth-century French
Baroque. The interior design follows the eclectic practice of decorating each main
room in a different style.

The New Mikhailovsky Palace is a more exuberant piece of work, combining
different stylistic elements. Built in 1857–1861 on Palace Quay for grand duke
Mikhail Nikolaevich, the structure is horizontally segmented by string courses
into three floors. Shtakenshneider provided a sense of depth to the facade by
designing a central projection with attached Corinthian columns, caryatids, and a
plethora of cornices and pediments. The statuary was sculpted in terra cotta by
David Jensen, one of Shtakenshneider's closest collaborators. The interior (particularly the second-floor state rooms) was richly decorated in a fashion similar to
that elsewhere in Europe during the period of eclecticism.

HISTORICAL MUSEUM. MOSCOW

The revival of interest in medieval Russian architecture in the 1860s and 1870s
reflected a growing interest in the country's cultural roots before the reign of Peter
the Great. The Historical Museum (1874–1883) is the most imposing and one of the
earliest examples of the Russian Revival style. The museum was intended to
express Russian historical consciousness on a site in the shadow of the Kremlin

Moscow   Historical Museum. 1874–83

walls, and the winning design reflected the monuments on Red Square (The Kremlin towers, and the Cathedral of the Intercession), as well as various sixteenth- and seventeenth-century monuments in elsewhere in Moscow. After a prolonged competition the project was awarded to Vladimir Shervud (Sherwood; of English descent), a graduate, in 1857, of the Moscow School of Painting and Sculpture. During his early years as an art student he became acquainted with a group of Moscow intellectuals and artists identified with the Slavophile movement.

In creating an emblem of national identity, Shervud incorporated as many historical references as possible. His design incorporates sixteenth- and seventeenth-century decorative motifs, with little of the sculpted plasticity of medieval architecture. In Shervud's design, each facade is a balanced surface, with projecting porches and towers and medieval decorative elements in bold relief. The pedagogic intent of the design pervades the interior halls, designed and decorated by a collective of artists (including Viktor Vasnetsov) and historians, who chose decorative materials appropriate to the various ages of Russian history and prehistory.

ABRAMTSEVO ESTATE. NEAR SERGIEV POSAD

In 1870 Savva Mamontov, a wealthy Moscow entrepreneur and railroad magnate, purchased the Abramtsevo estate from a daughter of Sergei Aksakov, whose leading role in the Slavophile movement had made Abramtsevo a haven for writers and intellectuals. Mamontov, in turn, created a center for the arts and crafts revival in Russia and attracted a diverse group of painters, sculptors, musicians, and other artists. With such a breadth of interests, the Abramtsevo community had a major influence on architecture and design. The most significant architectural work at Abramtsevo is the church, dedicated to the Icon of the Savior "not created by hand" (*nerukotvornyi*). Although of modest dimensions, it has become legendary in Russian art history—the realization of a artistic synthesis by a group dedicated to preserving art in the spiritual life of the people. The design of the Abramtsevo church derived not from the Byzantine or seventeenth-century Muscovite styles, but from the less grandiose traditions of medieval Novgorod and Pskov.

Viktor Vasnetsov, a painter of historical and semimythical subjects from the Russian past, made the final design for the church, constructed in 1881–1882. There are few "quotations" in this building: the exaggerated contours, the large curved segmented window on the south wall, and the carved limestone details do not reproduce with archaeological precision the small churches of Novgorod or Pskov—which in any event had been rebuilt extensively over the centuries. Yet the deeper structural similarity is recognizable, presented without the decorative detail that cluttered most examples of the Russian revival style.

The decoration of the interior and the design of the furnishings involved not only V. Polenov and Vasnetsov but also the painters Ilia Repin and Apollonary Vasnetsov (Viktor's brother), Elena Polenova, the sculptor Mark Antokolsky, and Savva Mamontov's wife, Elizaveta, who played an important role in the

Abramtsevo estate   Church of the Icon of the Savior. 1881–82. South view.

Abramtsevo crafts circle. Ten years after the church was completed Vasnetsov added a chapel on the north facade, where in 1892 Mamontov's invalid son Andrei was buried. In 1918 Savva Mamontov was buried in the same chapel.

UPPER TRADING ROWS. MOSCOW

The rebuilding of the Upper Trading Rows combined the Russian Revival style with advanced technology applied on a scale unprecedented in Russian civil architecture. Its site, facing the Kremlin, had been occupied by a neoclassical trading arcade constructed by Osip Bove after the 1812 fire. In 1888 a private company was formed to rebuild the complex, and the project was awarded to the Petersburg architect Aleksandr Pomerantsev. He derived his plan from the galleria, or *passage*, which had been used elsewhere in Europe as well as in Russia for retail trade throughout the nineteenth century. Yet nothing equalled the size of the new Upper Trading Rows, with its 1,000 to 1,200 shops. While the design of this many units with proper access, illumination, and ventilation required a commitment to new technological methods, the location of the Trading Rows demanded a structure whose style would reflect that of the historic monuments on Red Square.

Considerable ingenuity was required to reconcile the historicist facade with the commercial function of the interior, which dispensed with the Russian style in favor of Renaissance detail for the three parallel arcades that extend the length of the complex. Each arcade has three levels, with rows of shops on the first and sec-

Moscow   Upper Trading Rows. 1889–93

Moscow   Upper Trading Rows. Interior.

St. Petersburg   Church of the Resurrection on the Blood. South facade, detail.

ond and offices on the third. Illumination is provided by arched skylights, whose design ranks among the remarkable achievements of civil engineering in Russia during the nineteenth century. (Each weighs some 819 metric tons and has over 20,000 panes of glass). That the enormous Trading Rows functioned is a tribute both to the design of one of Russia's greatest civil engineers, Vladimir Shukhov (1853–1939) and to the technical proficiency of Russian architecture at the end of the century.

CHURCH OF THE RESURRECTION ON THE BLOOD. ST. PETERSBURG

In St. Petersburg, one of the few notable examples of the Russian Revival style is the Church of the Resurrection on the Blood (1883–1907), built on the site of Alexander II's assasination by radical populists in 1881. The design by Alfred Parland bears a superficial resemblance to St. Basil's in Moscow. Although incongruous in the setting of neoclassical Petersburg, the church presents a striking, festive image on the Griboedov Canal. Both the interior and exterior are distinguished by extensive mosaics designed by prominent artists such as Viktor Vasnetsov and produced by the A. A. Frolov firm.

11. TWENTIETH CENTURY

HOTEL METROPOLE. MOSCOW

Commissioned by the Petersburg Insurance Society to provide Moscow with a hotel that would meet international standards of design and luxury, the Metropole had a complicated construction history. Even the winning design of William Walcot was substantially modified—in certain respects almost beyond recognition—before work began in 1899. During the five years of construction, other architects were involved in the project, most notably Lev Kekushev, who supervised the construction and added a number of elements of his own.

There are many aspects of the Metropole that define it as a landmark of the style moderne. Although it has elements of horizontal and vertical emphasis, and a large arched panel at the center of the main facade, the facade itself contains little reference to the order system. The new style developed a concept of tectonics in which structural mass could be shaped without reference to illusionistic supporting elements. Texture and material acquired the dominant expressive role, exemplified at the Metropole by the progression from an arcade with stone facing on the ground floor to the upper floors in plaster over brick, with inset windows lacking any decorative frame. The central two stories are contained within two horizontal strips formed by wrought-iron balconies; vertical accents—both functional and decorative—are provided by glass bays in the center and at the corners of the main facade.

Paradoxically, this new relation between structure and material at the Metropole enabled the architect to use the facade as a ground upon which other art forms could be displayed, such as the plaster frieze by Nikolai Andreev on the theme "The Four Seasons" (along the fourth floor), and seven ceramic panels designed by Aleksandr Golovin above the fifth story. Most prominently, the great arch at the center of the main facade contains the ceramic panel "The Princess of Dreams," designed by Mikhail Vrubel. It is significant that both Vrubel and Golovin had been active in the Abramtsevo community, whose commitment to the arts and crafts revival and to an integrated concept of structure and decoration are so largely displayed at the Metropole.

Moscow   Hotel Metropole.

STEPAN RIABUSHINSKY HOUSE. MOSCOW

Having earlier used gothic stylization as a path to structural innovation, Shekhtel moved to a radically modern idiom in his house for Stepan Riabushinsky, near the Nikita Gates in central Moscow. Begun in 1900 and finished apparently by 1903, the Riabushinsky house displays a stylistic affinity with European modernism, yet it also incorporates the emphasis on decorative arts pioneered at Abramtsevo. Shekhtel's design uses contrasting elements, angular and sinuous, precise in line and complex in decorative form. The planes of yellow glazed brick provide a backdrop for an array of ornamental effects: large windows with bentwood details; wrought-iron railings in a fish-scale pattern; and, along the top of the walls, a mosaic frieze depicting irises on a background of clouds and azure sky. The sculpted forms of the porches on the side and front of the house suggest the entrance to a grotto. This reference to a submerged aquatic realm (possibly an allusion to Rimsky-Korsakov's opera *Sadko*) continues in the interior with the use of a pale color scheme dominated by green and blue, and with the repetition of aquatic motifs.

In the design of the central stairway Shekhtel approached the limits of the free-form possibilities of the style moderne. This space, extending the entire height of the house, serves as a core around which most of the rooms are grouped. The rooms themselves are modest in scale, and designed for intimate family life rather than public display. Yet the stairway is one of the most theatrical moments in Russian modernism, a stone wave cascading from the upper story to the bottom landing. At the foot of the stairs the wave surges to create a sculpted column capped with a lamp of stained glass and bronze in the form of an aquatic medusa.

Moscow   Stepan Riabushinsky house.

One can assume that this theatrical, "decadent" display reflected the desire to affirm a new cultural identity on the part of Stepan Riabushinsky; yet it must be remembered the at the Riabushinskys adhered to a conservative Old Believer sect of Russian Orthodoxy, as did a number of Moscow's prominent merchants. Not until after 1905 were the various Old Believer sects given official permission to construct places of worship, and Shekhtel acknowledged the private nature of this religious schism by designing a house chapel, with its separate staircase, at the back of the structure above the second story. Here, in contrast to the main part of the interior, the colors are boldly stated: red and gold for the dome and penden-

Moscow   Stepan Riabushinsky house. Plan.

Moscow   Stepan Riabushinsky house. Interior.

tives over a dark, patterned wall. These are the colors of medieval Russian icons, which Riabushinsky collected, and they are applied in a setting sensitive to religious tradition as well as aesthetically innovative.

PERTSOV APARTMENT HOUSE. MOSCOW

The close relation between material and design in Russian folk traditions received a renewed interpretation in the "neo-Russian" variant of the style moderne, which strove for an aesthetic transformation of the urban milieu. These possibilities were thoroughly explored by the artist Sergei Maliutin in his design for the apartment house of N. P. Pertsov at Prechistenka Quay (1905–1907). Maliutin used ceramic panels and other ornamentation based on exaggerated, abstract representations of folk art. Maliutin's sketch for the building masked the basic structure with a panoply of steeply pitched roofs, towers, elaborately decorated balconies and window surrounds, and large ceramic panels as well as unusual door and window openings. Maliutin intended to reproduce the asymmetry of the medieval *teremok*, a word that includes the concepts of "tower" and "chambers." The ideal proved beyond reach, however, and Maliutin's original design was considerably modified by Nikolai Zhukov, the architect who constructed the building. In an attempt to adapt the *teremok* to an actual living area, he designed the interior of the Pertsovs' own apartment with stylized carving, patterned wall designs, and hand-crafted furniture in the traditional crafts style.

Moscow   Pertsov apartment house.

SINGER BUILDING. ST. PETERSBURG

Among the many landmarks along Nevsky Prospekt, none is more noticeable than the building constructed for the Russian headquarters of the Singer Sewing Machine Company (1902–1904), located at the corner formed by the Catherine Canal. Its architect, Pavel Siuzor, was known not only for prodigious output (some 100 original projects and reconstructions, of which over 60 are extant), but also for his ability to adapt to stylistic and technical innovations.

The Singer Building, for example, contains something approaching a skeletal structural system, although not the steel frame of the type widely used in America. The exterior facades are supported with a ferro-concrete and brick frame, while the interior floors (also reinforced concrete) rest on iron columns.

By surfacing the arcade of the first two floors with rusticated blocks of polished red granite, and using a lighter, gray granite for the upper stories, Siuzor created a visual base for the structure, which rises in granite-surfaced piers and glass window shafts that extend from the third to the sixth floors in a secondary arcade pattern. The plate-glass windows, divided by two mullions, reach from floor to ceiling; and within the glass shafts, the base of each of the floors is marked by a spandrel and a bronze balcony rail with art nouveau tracery. The culminating element of the building is the elongated metal-ribbed and glass cupola at whose summit two female figures support a globe with the Singer logo. The glass-enclosed cupola and globe were illuminated for advertising purposes; and since they were not considered a usable part of the structure, the Singer Company could exceed

St. Petersburg Singer Building.

the height restrictions on Nevsky Prospekt. No other foreign enterprise in Russia had so visible an architectural presence.

GERMAN EMBASSY. ST. PETERSBURG

The inspiration for the reduced, "stripped" classicism in Petersburg architecture after 1910 derives not so much from the proliferation of varieties of the neoclassical revival, but rather from the monumental design by Peter Behrens for the new German Embassy (1911–12) on St. Isaac's Square. His contribution to this key site in central Petersburg is all the more remarkable for the difficult, trapezoidal site on which the embassy is situated. Behrens' solution was to create in effect two independent, yet joined, structures, surfaced in rough-hewn red granite. The main part, facing St. Isaac's Square and containing the embassy's state and reception rooms, is defined on the exterior by a horizontal frame of pilasters, attic, and base. By eliminating the acute corner angle, Behrens attached a second rectangular structure—extending along the side street and containing consular offices and staff quarters—at an angle to the main facade. This arrangement joined the two parts, and yet left each a discrete unit. In contemporary criticism on the building, its integrity of design and unity were associated with an absence of architectural ornamentation.

HOTEL ASTORIA. ST. PETERSBURG

A more severe form of late imperial neoclassicism characterizes Hotel Astoria by Fedor Lidval on St. Isaac's Square (1911–1912), a six-story building with a few highly visible decorative elements, such as the classical urns and channeled

St. Petersburg   German Embassy.

St. Petersburg Astoria Hotel.

pilasters along the austere granite facade. Lidval also created a number of prominent apartment buildings with a sensitive yet sparse application of classical and Renaissance detail.

DELOVOI DVOR OFFICE COMPLEX. MOSCOW

The adaptation of the neoclassical revival to the needs of modern functional design in commercial architecture before the First World War are best demonstrated in Ivan Kuznetsov's Business Court (Delovoi dvor, 1912–1913), a hotel and office complex located on New Square. The initiator of the project was Nikolai Vtorov, once of the most enterprising of Moscow's capitalists and, in the words of a contemporary observer, "the first to break the age-old traditions in favor of a rational and intelligent organization of commercial business." Vtorov located his project just beyond the Kitai-gorod wall in the heart of Moscow's commercial district, and he stipulated an advanced construction design. The plan included an elongated hotel in three attached segments and a trapezoidal office building for wholesale trade—each five to six stories in height.

Kuznetsov complied with the functional requirements in his ferroconcrete structure, but he also provided a neoclassical "cover" to mitigate the austerity of the design on the exterior and to provide a suitably imposing frame for the main entrances. The corner wedge of the hotel entrance on New Square is marked a neoclassical rotunda with Corinthian columns and dome, and the main point of entry to the office block displays a Corinthian portico and pediment hovering

Moscow Delovoi Dvor office complex.

over the entrance arch. This decorative flourish stands in contrast to the side facades of the building, which are altogether without ornamentation and display the orthogonal grid design with glazed infill characteristic of a new rationalist aesthetic.

IZVESTIIA BUILDING. MOSCOW

The unadorned geometric emphasis of Constructivist buildings erected in Moscow in the late 1920s and early 1930s is evident in Grigory Barkhin's building for the newspaper *Izvestiia* (1927). Using a grid with glass infill, Barkhin adopts a angular approach that offers no concession to decorative motifs. Both the horizontal and vertical lines are emphasized by a series of simple balconies, placed asymmetrically on the facade and in dynamic contrast to the four circular windows of the top story. The circle and square dominate here as clearly as they do in avantgarde set designs by Varvara Stepanova. Although traditional in its use of loadbearing brick walls, the building presented a modern front symbolizing the new order proclaimed by *Isvestiia*.

ZUEV CLUB. MOSCOW

One of the most durable of Constructivist buildings is Zuev Workers' Club, built by Ilia Golosov in 1927–1929. Graduated from the Moscow School of Painting, Sculpture, and Architecture in 1912, Golosov began his career before the revolution with designs in a predictable Neoclassical revival style. In the early 1920s he taught with Melnikov at VKhUTEMAS, and, like Melnikov, built or projected a number of wooden exhibition pavilions. At the same time he produced rather

Moscow   Izvestiia Building. 1927

eclectic sketches for competitions such as the Moscow Palace of Labor project (1922–23), with the arched roof of its central auditorium suggesting the shape of a dynamo. By 1925 Golosov's acceptance of Constructivist principles became markedly evident in a number of large office building designs, streamlined and reduced to a balance of rectilinear elements. The Zuev Club, however, was built with atypical concern for the integrity of the design, despite its complex contours. Many such clubs were built in the late twenties and thirties, and in the most pragmatic sense they were intended to provide a meeting and recreational space for both workers and professionals (whose alternative might have been the tavern). On the level of ideology, the workers' clubs provided an opportunity for the integration of architecture and social politics in the creation of communal structures.

The Zuev Club has been shabbily maintained, but the vigor of Golosov's concept has not diminished. The large corner cylinder, containing a stairwell enclosed in glass, rises through a rectangular extension of one of the upper floors. The resulting contrast of shapes epitomizes constructivist architecture, both in its display of steel, glass, and concrete, and in its massing of sharply defined volumes. The organization of interior space at the Zuev Club focuses on the staircase cylinder, whose wall of glass not only illuminates the interior, but also highlights the radial construction of the reinforced concrete beams beneath the upper landing.

Moscow Zuev Club. 1927–29

RUSAKOV CLUB. MOSCOW

Although unaffiliated with any particular faction in the avant garde, Konstantin Melnikov developed a distinctive modern idiom in his buildings for Moscow in the 1920s. The best-known example of Melnikov's bold shaping of structure is his Rusakov Club design (1927–1929) for the Union of Municipal Workers. It is the most dramatic of the workers' clubs, with its three cantilevered wedges plunging toward a point at the rear of the building. The effect of the three massive projections, separated by glass shafts in the front, is not only visually striking but functional as well, in providing a slope for the seats of the theater within. The building has been called "expressionist," and it indeed proclaims of itself more loudly than most other structures of the period. In the 1990s, the Rusakov Club, like many other workers' clubs, has lost previous sources of support and is now in a state of disrepair that could ultimately threaten the structure.

NARKOMFIN APARTMENT HOUSE. MOSCOW

One of the most visionary examples of the functional aesthetic is Moisei Ginzburg's the apartment house for the People's Commissariat of Finance (Narkomfin, 1928–1930), designed in collaboration with Ivan Milinis. In addition

Moscow   Rusakov Club. 1927–29

Moscow   Narkomfin apartment house. 1928–30

to his theoretical works establishing the principles of Constructivism in architecture, Ginzburg contributed greatly in the 1920s to the development of new concepts of housing, with particular emphasis on the social aspects of modern communal housing. Although in the debate over the feasibility of "de-urbanization" as opposed to greater urban concentration Ginzburg had stated his support for decentralization, his housing designs could achieve a massive scale—as in his 1925 project for a textile workers' apartment building (not built).

The smaller scale of the Narkomfin building (intended for 200 residents) contributed only marginally to a solution for resolving the urban housing crisis, but it illustrates admirably Ginzburg's statements on the necessary interdependence of aesthetics and functional design, "from the interior to the exterior." Built to contain apartments, as well as dormitory rooms arranged in a communal living system, the interior was meticulously designed, like that of many constructivist buildings. The main structure, adjoined at one end by a large block for communal services, rested on pilotis (now enclosed); and the structure culminated in an open frame solarium. The front, or east, facade of the building is defined by the sweeping horizontal lines of window strips and, on the lower floors, of connecting balconies.

The horizontality of the Narkomfin east facade, which follows the design of the straight interior corridors (facing the morning sun and suitable for calisthenics) along the length of the building, exists in counterpoint to the split-level design of the apartments themselves, which are marvels of spatial ingenuity. The complexity of this arrangement is delineated with greater clarity on the west facade: the floors are grouped in strips of two, and each end of the facade is marked by a stairwell shaft. The effect is austere, yet impressive in rhythm and balance.

GOVERNMENT APARTMENT HOUSE. MOSCOW

During the transitional period of the first Five-Year Plan (1928–1932), the functionalist aesthetic still influenced form, as exemplified in the enormous Moscow apartment complex known as the Government House on Serafimovich Street, designed by Boris Iofan with the assistance of Dmitry Iofan. Like many of the leading Soviet architects, Boris Iofan had traveled extensively in Italy, whose architecture he much admired. Returning to the Soviet Union in 1924, Iofan designed workers' housing in Moscow and the provinces until 1927, when he began work on the Government House, which was far larger than other experimental housing projects such as Ginzburg's Narkomfin building, under construction at the same time.

Located diagonally from the Kremlin across the Moscow River and Intended for use by the upper echelons of the party and government (the Central Committee of the party and the Council of People's Commissars), the complex was in fact a small city, three hectares in size and containing some 500 apartments, as well as a library, a gymnasium, a club, and an array of services and shops for the elite. Iofan accommodated these many functions within an ensemble of several buildings, constructed of a ferroconcrete skeleton with brick infill. Despite the uniformity of the fenestration and the lack of ornament, the project possessed its own "skyline," with setback roof structures; and the arrangement of three interior courtyards between the buildings (connected by enclosed passages raised on pilotis) pro-

Moscow   Government Apartment House. 1927–31

vided further variety to the design. The side facing the Moscow River on the Bersenevka Quay was symmetrically planned, with apartment towers flanking the facade of the club (later converted to a variety theater) and all linked by a large stripped colonnade symbolizing the structure's relation to the neoclassical architecture of central Moscow to the north across the river. Despite its constructivist aspects, the Government House already shows a turning toward classicizing elements, such as the general symmetry of its design and the use of colonnades. By the time of its completion in 1931 (work on the interior continued several more years because of technical difficulties), Iofan had embarked on the path of classicist monumentality.

TSENTROSOIUZ BUILDING. MOSCOW

Ginzburg's implementation of his concept of functionalism for the Narkomfin project demonstrated how closely such works were related to contemporary architecture in the rest of Europe. The closest affinity is with Le Corbusier's notion of the Unité d'Habitation. Le Corbusier and Ginzburg were personally acquainted, and in 1927 the French architect was included on the board of *Contemporary Architecture*, edited by Ginzburg and Aleksandr Vesnin. The following year Le Corbusier made the first of his three visits to the Soviet Union (the last in 1930). Le Corbusier's active collaboration in Russian architecture involved enormous conceptual projects that remained unrealized.

His enduring legacy, however, was the design for the headquarters for the Central Union of Consumer Societies (Tsentrosoiuz, 1929–1936). Assisted by his

Moscow   Tsentrosoiuz Building. 1929–36

cousin Pierre Jeanneret, and the Soviet architect Nikolai Kolli, Le Corbusier succeeded in completing the building on the intended scale, but without many of its planned technical refinements, such as an advanced system of circulating cooled or heated air through the double-glazed facade. Only eight stories tall, the building is an impressive mass composed of three elongated blocks. The center block is set back from Kirov Street, while the other two flank it in a perpendicular arrangement extending to the street line. Two of the blocks are sheathed in a glass curtain wall, framed in red tufa; and the central block rests on pilotis—now enclosed, although a restoration is supposed to return the ground floor to a semblance of its original appearance. The rear of the building contains an auditorium and club space. The main components of the interior are connected by spiral ramps.

APARTMENT HOUSE FOR THE LENINGRAD SOVIET. LENINGRAD

In 1931–1935, Igor Fomin and Evgeny Levinson designed an apartment complex for use by the Leningrad Soviet in the fashionable pre-revolutionary Petrograd District, on the bank of the Karpovka River near Kamennoostrovsky Prospekt (subsequently renamed after Kirov). With an open passageway supported by granite columns in the center of the curved facade, the design echoes the work of Ginzburg and, especially, of Le Corbusier. A stylobate of gray granite provides a base for the rest of the structure, whose facade is coated in artistic concrete with a scored surface. The careful attention to such details of architectural and decorative design are unusual for this period and indicate the privileged status of the city bureaucrats for whom the structure was built. With their balconies and wide windows overlooking the wooded river bank, some of the building's 76 apartments reached a size of six rooms (on two levels)—this at a time when desirable prerevolutionary apartments of similar size were being subdivided for the use of one family to a room.

WORKERS' CLUB OF THE PROLETARIAN DISTRICT. MOSCOW

Among the Constructivist architects, the most productive were the Vesnin brothers, Leonid, Viktor, and Alexander, all of whom completed their education in Petersburg before the war. In 1925, Alexander and Viktor Vesnin, together with

Leningrad   Apartment house of the Leningrad Soviet. 1931–35

Moscow   Workers' Club of the Proletarian District. 1932–37

Moisei Ginzburg, founded the Constructivist organization OSA (Society of Contemporary Architects). With the quickening tempo of construction during the late 1920s, the Vesnins were engaged in major projects such as the hydroelectric dam across the Dnieper River. The culminating achievement in the Vesnins' Constructivist oeuvre was an extension of the concept of the workers' club, conceived as a large complex of three buildings to serve the social needs of the Proletarian District, a factory and workers' district in southeast Moscow. The site overlooked the Moscow River and was adjacent to the Simonov Monastery, part of whose walls were razed in the course of constructing the project. Yet the largest part of the ensemble, a theater with a circular hall designed to seat 4,000, was never built. The central element, however, was the club building itself, built between 1931 and 1937.

Despite the death of Leonid Vesnin in 1933 and the increasing intensity of attacks on modern architecture, the Vesnins persevered in work on the club. Viktor and Aleksandr Vesnin considered the Proletarian Region club one of their most significant works, not only for its union of functions—a 1,000-seat theater, ballroom, meeting halls, exhibition space—but also for the way in which form followed function and space flowed effortlessly from one component to another. In the club building the Vesnins' fluency was reflected on the exterior in such details as the contours of the large rounded bay window over the entrance to the auditorium, and a semi-circular conservatory extending from the river facade. The club also included a small astronomy observatory, whose design added to the variety of the building's upper structure.

STATE LENIN LIBRARY. MOSCOW

One of the clearest examples of the amalgamation of functionalism and incipient monumentality occurred with the construction of the main library of the Soviet Union, the Lenin Library. The competition for the project, in 1928, produced a number of avant-garde proposals, but the project was awarded to a more conservative, eclectic design by Vasily Shchuko and Vladimir Gelfreikh. To be sure, the classicizing elements, such as the colonnade and portico, were very much in the modernized, stripped manner; and the statuary above the cornice of the main structure was an elaboration that evolved over the extended period of construction, which embodied the transition from modernism to conservative forms. The library was not completed until 1940, and the outfitting of the main reading rooms continued well after the war. The statuary, the frieze above the main portico, and the bronze reliefs of noted thinkers between the pylons of the facade signaled a return to a traditional (Renaissance and classical) synthesis of monumental art forms as a means of expressing—or manipulating—ideological content in architecture.

APARTMENT BUILDING, 16 MARX PROSPEKT

In the early 1930s it became clear that retrospective architectural styles would play a major role in the new monumentalism. The new concept of "socialist realism" had to be given content, which by the Stalinist dialectic was to be derived not from

Moscow   State Lenin Library. 1928–40

an innovative—if occasionally monotonous—functionalism (now labeled formal-
ism), but from conservative neoclassical and neo-Muscovite styles. Among the for-
mulators of the style were architects such as Ivan Zholtovsky, who had never
abandoned the pre-revolutionary Renaissance, classicist origins of his career. In
1934 Zholtovsky constructed a seven-story apartment building, at 16 Marx
Prospekt (facing the northwest wall of the Kremlin) in a hypertrophied neoclassical revival style. Its gargantuan attached columns reached five stories, and culminated in composite capitals.

Moscow   Apartment building, 16 Marx Prospekt. 1934

Moscow   Hotel Moskva. 1930–35

HOTEL MOSKVA. MOSCOW

Aleksei Shchusev's prolific career illustrates the major changes in architectural style that accompanied political shifts in the Soviet regime. In the late 1920s he had designed the building of the Commissariat of Agriculture (1929–1933), one of the more notable buildings in the modern style. Soon thereafter, Shchusev applied an eclectic medley of classicizing elements to his design of the capital's new showcase hotel, the "Moskva" (1930–1935), on the site of the former Okhotnyi Riad (Huntsman's Row) to the northeast of the Kremlin. The project was intended to demonstrate that Soviet architects, craftsmen, and technology could be used to produce a hotel equaling the highest international standards. Therefore much attention was given to the furnishings and decorative details of the main halls and the deluxe suites—a precedent that would be expanded to lavish extent after the war.

COUNCIL OF PEOPLE'S COMMISSARIATS. MOSCOW

Facing the side (north) facade of the Hotel Moskva was a more austere product of the new monumentalism, the building for the central Soviet administrative apparatus: the Council of Labor and Defense, subsequently the Council of People's

Moscow   Council of People's Commissariats. 1932–36

Commissariats, and still later Gosplan (the main state planning agency). After 1993, it was converted for use by the Duma, or legislature, of the Russian Federation. The primary architect, Arkady Langman, had already completed the Dinamo Stadium in the north of Moscow (1927, with L. Cherikover), as well as a building for the Commissariat of Interior Affairs (1932–1933) near Ivan Fomin's building for the Dinamo Society (also connected with the state police). The council building (1932–1936) is of relatively low height—ten stories—in relation to the length of its facade, and this horizontality is massively confirmed by the unadorned cornice that caps the building and from which rises a low attic. The vertical pylons that segment the facade convey the impression of a barred surface, and for both its supporters and detractors the building has represented the epitome of the centralized and seemingly omnipotent administrative culture.

MOSCOW STATE UNIVERSITY.

The unprecedented destruction visited upon the Soviet Union by the Second World War (approximately thirty percent of the national wealth) ushered in a final era of monumental construction projects, as cities such as Stalingrad, Smolensk, Minsk, Kharkov, and Kiev were rebuilt from the ground up. Architecture reached still greater heights of bombast, epitomized in the late 1940s and early 1950s by the rise of "Stalinist gothic" buildings. Cities from Warsaw to Tashkent exhibited details of the style; but the center remained Moscow, where eight tower buildings were designed with a pastiche of decorative motifs adapted from neo-Gothic skyscrapers in New York, as well as classicizing elements from the 1930s (such as the unbuilt Palace of Soviets), and crowned with motifs from sixteenth and seventeenth-century Muscovite architecture.

Ultimately, only seven of these skyscrapers were built in Moscow. Their placement defined certain key points in the topography of the city—a role emphasized by their large spires, redolent both of medieval bell towers and of the spires of Petersburg. The use of a vertical dominant in organizing a low array of surrounding structures had long been a feature of Russian architecture; and although not all of these "tall buildings" were originally designed with the spires, they obtained them in the final designs as a recognition of their symbolic and visual role in a city that retained a largely horizontal, "communal" profile.

The most imposing of all was the new central building of Moscow State University (1949–1953; by Lev Rudnev, Pavel Abrosimov, and Aleksandr Khriakov) on Lenin Hills, overlooking the Moscow River and the central part of the city to the north. The main architect, Lev Rudnev, had played an important role in defining Soviet monumentalism with buildings such as the M. V. Frunze Military Academy (1932–1937; in collaboration with V. O. Munts). The new university building represents a later, flamboyant stage of totalitarian architecture, and was designed as a self-contained and tightly regulated community, a melding of utopian notions of communism with the unparalleled elitism of the late Stalinist period. Although it suggests elements of early Manhattan skyscraper design, its vast and sprawling symmetry is unique. Wasteful of interior space and bombastic, the Moscow University tower does exactly what it was intended to do: dominate the city.

Moscow State University   1949–53

NEW ARBAT (KALININ PROSPEKT). MOSCOW

The most prolific practitioner of post-war Soviet modernism was Mikhail Posokhin, who had collaborated in the design of the Stalinist apartment tower on Insurrection Square but then shifted adroitly into the new functionalism, interpreted in Moscow on a monumental scale appropriate to the confidence of the Sputnik era. His design for the Kremlin Palace of Congresses (1959–1961, in collaboration with A. Mndoiants and others) had the appearance of a modern concert hall (one of its uses) of huge proportions, whose marble-clad rectangular outline was marked by narrow pylons—also faced with white marble—and multi-storied shafts of plate glass.

Posokhin subsequently adapted the international modern style, with its glass and aluminum facades, to industrialized methods of construction in the creation of such ensembles as Kalinin Prospekt (1964–1969; also known as the New Arbat), extending westward from the Kremlin and Arbat Square. Its identical towers and shopping complexes provided the capital with the facade of cosmopolitan prosperity, but the project inflicted great damage on the original Arbat district.

Moscow   New Arbat.

APARTMENT HOUSE OF NEW LIVING. MOSCOW

Even the radical ideals of the "house-commune" of the 1920s returned in at least one project: the House of New Living (*dom novogo byta*; 1969; N. Osterman, A. Petrushkova, et al.), with 812 apartments designed primarily for young married students who were not yet prepared for the rigors of household life and could make use of the project's centralized services. However, many of the technological marvels remained on the drawing board, and the project proved hardly more successful than its predecessors; it was soon converted to a graduate student dormitory for Moscow State University and other institutions.

CHILDREN'S MUSICAL THEATER. MOSCOW

Although post-Stalinist architectural design has in general remained subordinate to mass construction techniques, there are projects that ingeniously exploit these limitations, such as the Children's Musical Theater near Moscow State University (1979). Wishing to create a monolithic structure of simple geometric contrasts but unable to use the techniques of poured, textured concrete that characterize Western "brutalism," the architects Aleksandr Velikanov and V.

Moscow   Apartment House of New Living. 1969

Krasilnikov sheathed the facade in textured stone and concrete panels, decorated with fanciful sculpture from children's fables to provide relief within the horizontal mass of the building. The seams that mark prefabricated architecture are here integrated into the rough surface, thus adapting standardized components to a sculpted design.

Moscow   Children's Musical Theater. 1979

Illustrated Architectural Elements

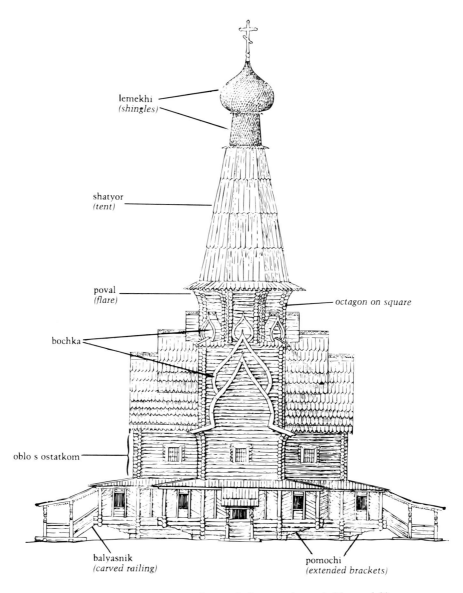

lemekhi
(shingles)

shatyor
(tent)

poval
(flare)

octagon on square

bochka

oblo s ostatkom

balyasnik
(carved railing)

pomochi
(extended brackets)

Church of the Presentation at Osinovo   (near Arkhangelsk)

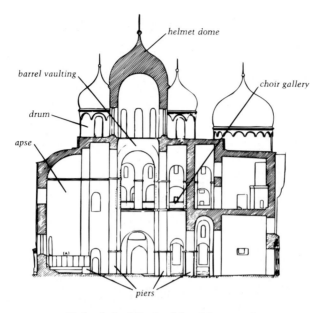

Cathedral of St. Sophia　Novgorod.

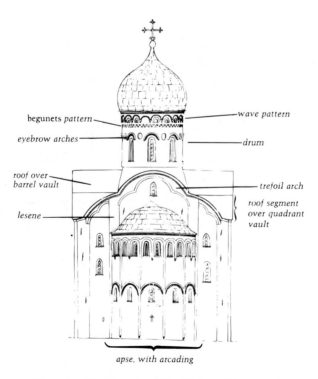

Church of St. Theodore Stratilates　Novgorod.

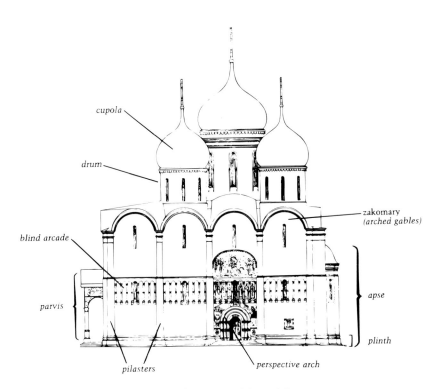

cupola

drum

*zakomary
(arched gables)*

blind arcade

apse

parvis

plinth

pilasters

perspective arch

Cathedral of the Dormition   Moscow.

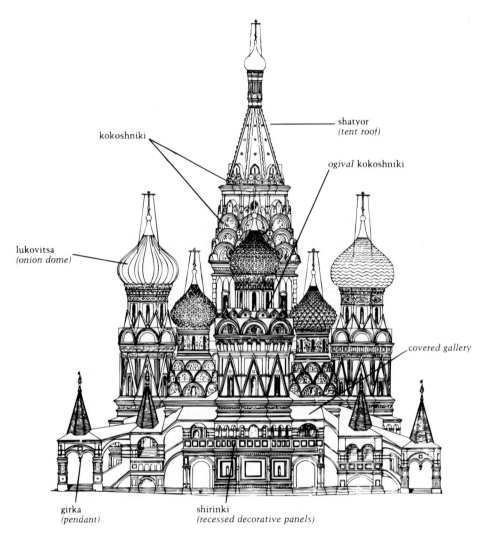

Cathedral of the Intercession (St. Basil's)   Moscow.

Index

(Bold italicized page numbers indicate photographs of designated buildings.)

A

Abramtsevo, 5, 205–206, 211, 212
   Church of the Icon of the Savior, 6, **_206_**
Abrosimov, Pavel, 230
Adam, Robert, 4
Aleksandrova Sloboda, 104, **_105_**
   Cathedral of the Intercession, 105
   Church of the Crucifixion, **_105_**
Aleksei Mikhailovich, tsar, 118, 120, 128
Alexander I, emperor, 180, 199
Alexander II, emperor, 209
Aleviz Novy, 2, 76, 108
Andreev, Nikolai, 211
Andrei Bogoliubsky, prince, 1, 49, 54
Anne, empress, 3
Antonio Friazin, 2
Argunov, Pavel, 179
Arkhangelsk
   Church of the Presentation at
      Osinovo, 235

B

Barkhin, Grigory, 7, 219
Basil (Vasily) I, grand prince, 67
Basil (Vasily) III, grand prince, 80, 93,
     94, 104, 107
Bazhenov, Vasily, 4, 5, 172, 176, 183
Behrens, Peter, 217

Benois, Nicholas, 202
Blank, Karl, 178
Bogoliubovo, 49–54
Bon Friazin, 2, 87
Boris Godunov, tsar, 87, 106–108
Bove, Osip, 5, 192, 207
Brenna, Vincenza, 4, 176, 188
Briullov, Aleksandr, 168
Briullov, Karl, 201
Bukhvostov, Yakov, 3, 137, 139, 143
Bykovsky, Michail, 5

C

Cameron, Charles, 4, 156, 173–176
Camporesi, Francesco, 178
Catherine II (the Great), empress, 4, 5,
     154, 156, 167, 171–174
Chernigov
   Cathedral of Saints Boris and Gleb,
      34, **_35_**
   Cathedral of the Transfiguration, 1,
      31, **_34_**
   Church of St. Paraskeva, 34, **_35_**, **_36_**
Chevakinsky, Savva, 4, 161–163, 166
Chiaveri, Gaetano, 152

D

Dmitry Donskoi, grand prince, 65, 81

E

Elizabeth, empress, 3, 156, 157, 158, 161
Erikhson, Adolf, 6
Ermolin, Vasily, 62, 71

F

Falconet, Etienne, 5
Ferapontov Monastery
   Cathedral of Nativity of the Virgin,
      67, *70*
   log Church of Deposition of the
      Robe, from Borodavo, 9, *10*
Fioravanti, Aristotle, 2, 71, 139
Fomin, Igor, 225
Fomin, Ivan, 230
Fontana, Giovanni Mario, 152
Frolov, A. A., 209
Fursov, P. I., 198

G

Gelfreikh, Vladimir, 227
Gilardi, Domenico, 5, 193
Ginzburg, Mosei, 7, 221, 223, 224, 225
Golitsyn, Boris, prince, 141
Golitsyn, Vasily, prince, 135
Golosov, Ilia, 7, 219
Golovin, Aleksandr, 211
Grigorev, Afanasy, 5, 194–195

H

Halloway, Christopher, 71
Hartmann, Viktor, 5

I

Iofan, Boris, 223
Istra
   Monastery of the Resurrection at
      New Jerusalem, 3, 118
   Cathedral of the Resurrection,
      118–120, *121–122*
   Church of the Entry into
      Jerusalem, *119*
Ivan III (the Great), grand prince of
   Moscow, 2, 71, 76

Ivan IV (the Terrible), tsar, 2, 91, 95,
   101, 104, 105, 117

J

Jensen, David, 204

K

Kaluga
   Zolotarev house, *180*, 181
Kavos, Albert, 192
Kazakov, Matvey, 5, 171, 173, 176,
      178, 193
Kazakov, Rodion, 5
Kazan, 95
   Siuiumbeki Tower, 131, *133*
Kizhi Island
   log Chapel of Archangel Michael,
      9, *13*
   log Church of the Resurrection of
      Lazarus, 9, *10*
   log Church of the Intercession, *22*,
      24, *25–26*
   log Church of the Transfiguration,
      21, *22–23*, 24
   log house, from Kleshcheila, *28–29*
   log house, from Monozero, *29*
Kekushev, Lev, 6, 211
Khriakov, Aleksandr, 230
Kiev
   Cathedral of Divine Wisdom (St.
      Sophia), 1, 31, *32*, *33*, 37
   Cathedral of the Dormition, Kiev
      Cave Monastery, 1
   Church of St. Andrew, 156
Kirillov
   St. Kirill-Belozersk Monastery, *122*
   Cathedral of the Dormition, 120
Klein, Roman, 6
Kokorinov, Aleksandr, 4, 165, 168
Kolli, Nikolai, 225
Kolomna
   Brusensky Monastery
      Church of the Dormition, 95, *96*
   Piatnitsky Gate, 94, *95*
Kon, Fedor, 2
Korobov, Ivan, 165, 185, 187

Kostroma, 196, *197*, 198
  log Church of the Transfiguration, from Spas-Vezhi, 11, *14*
  log house, *27*
Krasilnikov, V., 233
Kuznetsov, Ivan, 218

L

Langman, Arkady, 230
Le Blond, Jean Baptiste, 3, 153
Le Corbusier, 224–225
Levinson, Evgeny, 225
Lidval, Fedor, 6, 217–218
Lvov, Nikolai, 181

M

Mamontov, Savva, 5, 205–207
Maliutin, Sergei, 6, 215
Marco Friazin, 2, 71, 76
Mattarnovy, Georg, 3, 151–152
Melnikov, Konstantin, 7, 219, 221
Menshikov, Alexander, 143, 145, 152–153
Mikhail Fedorovich, tsar, 114
Mikhailov, Andrei, 192
Milinis, Ivan, 221
Mndoiants, A., 231
Monighetti, Ippolit, 156
Montferrand, Auguste, 5, 199
Moscow and environs
  Apartment Building, 16 Marx Prospekt, 227, *228*
  Apartment House of New Living, 232, *233*
  Baryshnikov (I. I.) house, 176, *177*
  Bell tower of Ivan the Great (Kremlin), 2, 87, *88*
  Bolshoi Theater, *192*
  Cathedral of the Annunciation (Kremlin), 199
  Cathedral of Archangel Michael (Kremlin), 2, 76, *77–78*, 108, 147
  Cathedral of the Dormition (Kremlin), 2, 71, *73–74*, 76, 101, 108, 140, 161, 237
  Cathedral of Intercession on the Moat (St. Basil's), 2, 94, 95–96, *97–100*, 209, 238
  Children's Musical Theater, 232, *233*
  Church of Archangel Gabriel (Menshikov Tower), 143, *144*, 145
  Church of the Ascension at Kolomenskoe, 2, 87, *89–91*, 93, 106
  Church of Christ the Redeemer, 5
  Church of the Decapitation of John the Baptist, 2, 91, *92–94*
  Church of the Intercession at Fili, 3, 140, *141–142*, 143
  Church of St. Nicholas in Khamovniki, 121, *123*
  Church of the Transfiguration at Ostrov, 105, *106*
  Church of the Transfiguration at Ubory, 3, 143
  Church of the Trinity in Nikitniki, 111, *112*
  Church of the Trinity in Ostankino, 123, *124*, 178
  Church of the Trinity at Troitskoe-Lykovo, 3
  Church of the Trinity at Viaziomy, 108, *109*
  Church of the Twelve Apostles (Kremlin), 117, *118*
  Council of People's Commissariats, 229, 230
  Delovoi Dvor (Business Court), 218, *219*
  Derozhinskaia house, 6
  Dinamo Stadium, 230
  Donskoi Monastery, 106
  Cathedral of Don Mother of God, *107*, 108
  Faceted Palace (Kremlin), 2, 71, 75, 76, 135, 199
  Frunze Military Academy, 230
  Government Apartment House, 223, *224*
  Great Kremlin Palace, 5, 199, *200*

Historical Museum, 6, 204, *205*
Hotel Metropole, 6, 211, *212*
Hotel Moskva, *229*
Izvestiia Building, 219, *220*
Kalinin Prospekt, 231, *232*
Kazan Railway Station, 131
Khrushchev (A. P.) house, 194, *195*, 196
Kremlin walls, 2, 5, 71, *72*, *75*, 95
Kremlin Palace of Congresses, 231
Lenin Library, 227, *228*
Marfino, estate, 5
Moscow University, 5, *193–194*
Moscow State University, 230, *231*
Muir and Mirrielees Department Store, 6
Museum of Fine Arts, 6
Narkomfin Apartment House, 221, *222*, 223
New Arbat, 231, *232*
Novodevichy Convent, 135
    Cathedral of the Smolensk Mother of God, 101, *102*, 103
    Church of the Dormition, 135
    Church of the Intercession, 136
    Church of the Transfiguration, 135, *136*
Old English Court, *117*
Ostankino palace, *178–179*, 180
Pashkov House, 5, 176, *177*
Pertsov apartment house, *215*
Petrovsky Transit Palace, *171*
Provision Warehouses, *196*
Riabushinsky (S. P.) house, 6, 212, *213–214*
Rusakov Club, 221, *222*
Savior-Andronikov Monastery
    Cathedral of the Savior, 67, *69–70*
Simonov Monastery, 227
Sukharev Tower, 3
Terem Palace (Kremlin), 199
Tretiakov Gallery, 6
Tsaritsyno, imperial estate, 5, *172–173*
Tsentrosoiuz Building, 224, *225*
Upper Trading Rows, 6, *207–208*, 209

Workers' Club of the Proletarian District, 225, *226*, 227
Zuev Club, 219–220, *221*
Mozhaisk
    Luzhetsky Monastery, 103
    Cathedral of the Nativity of the Virgin, *103*, 104
Munts, V. O., 230

N

Nicholas I, emperor, 5, 199
Nikitin, Gury, 117
Nikon, patriarch of Russian Orthodox church, 3, 118–119
Nizhnii Novgorod Stroganov Church of the Nativity, *frontispiece*
Novgorod and environs
    Antoniev Monastery
        Church of Nativity of the Virgin, 42, *44*
    Cathedral of Divine Wisdom (St. Sophia), 1, 37, *38–40*, 236
    Church of the Annunciation on the Trading Side, 83, *85*
    Church of Archangel Michael, 83, *85*
    Church of St. Theodore Stratilates, 2, 42, *45*, 236
    Church of Sts. Peter and Paul in Kozhevniki, *47*, 48
    Church of Sts. Boris and Gleb in Plotniki, 81, *83*
    Church of the Transfiguration on Elijah Street, 2, 45, *46*
    Khutyn Monastery
        Cathedral of the Transfiguration, *81–82*
    log Church of the Dormition, from Kuritsko, 11, *16*
    log Church of the Dormition, from Nikulino, 9, *11*
    log Church of the Nativity, from Peredki, 11, *17–18*
    log Church of St. Nicholas, from Miakishevo, 9, *14*
    log Church of St. Nicholas, from Tukholia, 9, *13*

log Church of St. Nicholas, from
Vysoky Ostrov, 11, *21*
log house, from Pyrishchi, *27*
Monastery of St. Nicholas at
Viazhishche, 131
Cathedral of St. Nicholas, 131,
133
Church of the Ascension, 134
Church of St. John the Divine, *134*
Yurev Monastery
Cathedral of St. George, 39, *41–43*

O

Orlov, Grigory, 167
Osterman, N., 232

P

Parland, Alfred, 6
Paul, emperor, 4, 175–176, 182
Pavlovsk
Palace, 4, *175*, 176
Temple of Friendship, 4
Pereslavl-Zalessky
Cathedral of the Transfiguration, 1,
49, *50*
Peter I (the Great), emperor, 3, 141,
147, 150, 185
Peter II, emperor, 153
Peterhof
Court Stables, 202
Palace, 3, *153*, 154
Petrok Malyi, 90
Petrushkova, A., 232
Philip, metropolitan, 71
Plekhanov, Dmitry Grigorev, 101, 125
Podolsk
Church of the Icon of the Sign at
Dubrovisty, 141, *143*
Polenov, Vasily, 206
Polenova, Elena, 206
Pomerantsev, Aleksandr, 6, 207
Posokhin, Mikhail, 231
Pospelov, Andrei, 150
Prokofiev, Ivan, 176
Pskov
Cathedral of the Trinity, 86

Church of the Epiphany, *85*, 86
Church of St. Nicholas, *86*, 87

Q

Quarenghi, Giacomo, 4, 178

R

Rastrelli, Bartolomeo Francesco, 3,
153–161
Repin, Ilia, 206
Riabushinsky, Stepan, 212–213
Riazan
Cathedral of the Dormition, 3, 137,
139
Rinaldi, Antonio, 4, 167
Ropet, Ivan, 5
Rossi, Carlo, 4, 188, 190
Rostov
Belfry, *79*, 129
Cathedral of the Dormition, 76, *79*,
80, 128, 131
Church of the Resurrection, *128*, 129
Church of St. John the Divine, *130*,
131, *132*
Church of the Savior on the Stores,
131
Red Chambers, *129*
Rudnev, Lev, 230

S

St. Petersburg
Academy of Arts, 165, *166*
Academy of Sciences, 4
Admiralty, 4, 185, *186*, 187, *188*
Alexander Nevsky Monastery, 3
Cathedral of the Trinity, 4, 168,
169, 192
Church of the Annunciation, 3
Alexandrine Theater, 5
Apartment House for the
Leningrad Soviet, 225, *226*
Bourse (Stock Exchange), 4, 184, *185*
Bronze Horseman, 5
Cathedral of the Kazan Mother of
God, 4, *182–183*, 184

Cathedral of St. Isaac, 5, 199,
    200–201, 202
Cathedral of St. Nicholas, 4, 161,
    162, 163
Cathedral of SS. Peter and Paul, 3,
    147, *148–149*, 150, 152
Cathedral of the Trinity
    (Izmailovsky), 190, *191*
Chesme Palace, 4, 170
Church of John the Baptist at
    Chesme, 4, *170*
Church of the Icon of the Savior, 5
Church of the Resurrection on the
    Blood, 6, *209*
Court Stables and church, 5, 190,
    191
General Staff Building, 5, 188, *189*,
    190
German Embassy, *217*
Gostinny Dvor, 4
Hermitage, 4
Hermitage Theater, 4
Hotel Astoria, 6, 217, *218*
Kunstkammer, 3, *151*, 152
Marble Palace, 4, 167, *168*
Mariinsky Palace, *203*
Menshikov Palace, *152*, 153
Mikhailovsky Castle, 4
Mikhailovsky Palace, 5, 188
Mining Insitute, 4
Moika Canal, 5
New Holland, 4, 165–166, *167*
New Mikhailovsky Palace, *204*
Palace Square, 5
Senate and Holy Synod, 5
Singer Building, 6, *216*
Smolny (Resurrection) Convent, 3,
    158, *160*, 161
Smolny Institute, 4
Stroganov Palace, 3, 156, *157*
Summer Palace of Elizabeth, 3
Summer Palace of Peter I, 3
Twelve Colleges Building, 3, *150*,
    151
Vasilevsky Island, 4, 151
Winter Palace, 3, 158, *159*, 165, 190
Savin, Sila, 117

Schädel, Gottfried Johann, 153
Schlüter, Andreas, 3, 151–152
Schwertfeger, Theodor, 152
Scotti, Carlo, 176
Sergiev Posad
    Trinity-St. Sergius Monastery, 3, 120
        Cathedral of the Dormition, 101
        Cathedral of the Trinity, 67, *68*
        Church of St. Sergius, 134, *135*
        Church of Sts. Zosima and
            Savvaty, 113, *114*
Serpukhov
    Church of the Trinity, 123, *125*
Shchedrin, Feodosy, 187
Shchuko, Vasily, 227
Shchusev, Alexsei, 7, 229
Shekhtel, Fedor, 6, 212–213
Sheremetev, Nikolai, 178
Shervud, Vladimir, 6, 205
Shestakov, Fedor, 196
Shtakenshneider, Andrey, 5, 203–204
Shubin, Fedot, 170
Shukhov, Vladimir, 6, 209
Siuzor, Pavel, 216
Smolensk, 2, 103
Solari, Pietro Antonio, 2, 71, 76, 131
Solovetsk Islands
    Monastery of the Transfiguration,
        113
Sophia, tsarevna, 135
Starov, Ivan, 4, 168–169
Startsev, Osip, 76
Stasov, Vasily, 5, 161, 190–192, 196,
    198
Stroganov, Alexander, 183
Stroganov, Sergei, 157
Suzdal
    Cathedral of Nativity of the Virgin,
        2, 60, *61–62*
    Convent of the Intercession, 80
        Cathedral of the Intercession, *80*
        Church of the Conception of St.
            Anne, 104
    log Church of St. Nicholas, from
        Potakino, 9, *12*
    log Church of the Transfiguration,
        from Kozliatevo, 11, *19*

Savior-Evfimy Monastery
    Church of the Dormition, *104*
Sysoevich, Jonah, metropolitan, 3, 128

T

Tarsia, Bartolomeo, 154
Teriaevo (see Volokolamsk)
Thomon, Jean Thomas de, 4, 184–185
Ton, Konstantin, 5, 199
Torzhok
    Cathedral of Sts. Boris and Gleb,
        181, 182
    log Church of the Ascension, *20*
Trezzini, Domenico, 3, 147, 150, 169
Trezzini, Giuseppe, 151
Trotsky, Noi, 7
Tsarskoe Selo
    Alexander Palace, 4
    Cameron Gallery, 4, 173, *174*
    Catherine Palace, 3, 4, 154, *155*, 156

U

Uglich
    Monastery of St. Aleksy
        Church of the Dormition, 111, *113*

V

Valeriani, Giuseppe, 154, 156
Vallin de la Mothe, Jean-Baptiste, 4,
        154, 165–166
Vanvitelli, Luigi, 167
Vasily (Basil) I, grand prince, 67
Vasily (Basil) III, grand prince, 80, 93,
        94, 104, 107
Vasnetsov, Apollonary, 206
Vasnetsov, Viktor, 6, 205, 206–207,
        209
Vesnin brothers, 7, 224, 225, 227
Veldten, Georg Friedrich, 4, 154, 161,
        170
Velikanov, Aleksandr, 232
Viazma
    Monastery of John the Baptist
        Church of the Hodigitria Icon,
            114, *115*, 116

Vitali, Ivan, 201
Vladimir and environs
    Cathedral of the Dormition, 2,
        54–56, *55*, 76
    Cathedral of St. Dmitry, 2, 56–60,
        57–59
    Church of Intercession on the Nerl,
        2, 49–54, *51–53*, 58
Vladimir, grand prince of Kiev, 1
Vladimir, prince of Novgorod, 37
Vologda
    Cathedral of St. Sophia (Divine
        Wisdom), 100, *101*
    log house, from Vnukovo, *28*
    Savior-Prilutsky Monastery, 81
        Cathedral of the Savior, 81, *84*
        log Church of the Dormition,
            from St. Alexander
            Kushtsky Monastery, 11, *15*
Volokolamsk
    St. Joseph-Volokolamsk Monastery
        at Teriaevo, 136
        Cathedral of the Dormition,
            137–138
Volotsky, Joseph, 136
Vrubel, Mikhail, 211
Voronikhin, Andrey, 4, 158, 183–184
Vorotilov, Stepan, 198
Vsevolod III, prince, 54, 56, 60
Vtorov, Nikolai, 218

W

Walcot, William, 6, 211

Y

Yaroslav the Wise, grand prince of
        Kiev, 1, 31, 37
Yaroslavl
    Church of the Epiphany, *127*, 128
    Church of John the Baptist at
        Tolchkovo, 124–125, *126*, 127,
        134
    Church of Prophet Elijah, *116*, 117
Yurev-Polskoy
    Cathedral of St. George, 2, 60, *62–63*

Yury Dmitrevich, prince of
    Zvenigorod, 65, 67
Yury Dolgoruky, grand prince, 1

Z

Zakharov, Andreian, 4, 185, 187–188
Zamaraev, Gavriil, 193
Zarudny, Ivan, 150

Zemtsov, Mikhail, 3, 152, 182
Zholtovsky, Ivan, 7, 228
Zhukov, Nikolai, 215
Zvenigorod
   Cathedral of the Dormition, 65,
     66
   Savva-Storozhevsky Monastery
    Cathedral of the Nativity of the
     Virgin, 65, *66*